HOM
MYSTICS

**Restoring Our Nation
with the Healing Wisdom
of America's Visionaries**

HOMEGROWN

MYSTICS

Restoring Our Nation
with the Healing Wisdom
of America's Visionaries

BRUCE EPPERLY

ANAMCHARA
BOOKS

ANAMCHARA BOOKS
Vestal, New York 13850
www.AnamcharaBooks.com

paperback ISBN: 978-1-62524-914-2
eBook ISBN: 978-1-62524-915-9

All Bible quotations, unless otherwise indicated, are from the New Revised Standard Version the Bible, copyright © 1989, National Council of the Churches of Christ in the United States of America. Used by permission. All rights reserved worldwide. The Bible quotation labeled WEB is from the World English Bible, which is in the public domain.

Unless otherwise indicated:

All quotations by Emerson are taken from *Essential Writings of Ralph Waldo Emerson* (New York: Modern Library, 2000). Quotations from Thoreau are from *Walden and Other Writings* (New York: Bantam Books, 1962). Quotes from Walt Whitman are taken from *The Complete Poems of Walt Whitman* (New York: Penguin, 2005). Quotations from Emily Dickinson are from *The Complete Poems of Emily Dickinson*, edited by Thomas Johnson (New York: Little Brown and Company, 1961). Quotations from John Woolman are taken from his journal, *A Journal of the Life, Gospel Labours, and Christian Experiences, of that Faithful Minister of Jesus Christ, John Woolman* (New York: Macmillan, 1903) and *The Writings of John Woolman* (Nashville, TN: Upper Room Books, 2000). Quotes from Ann Lee are taken from *The Communistic Societies of the United States* by Charles Nordhoff (1875), available online from SacredTexts.com. Black Elk's quotes are drawn from John G. Neihardt's *Black Elk Speaks* (Lincoln, NE: University of Nebraska Press, 1961). Quotations from John Muir are from his journals, which are included in *John Muir: Spiritual Writings*, edited by Tim Flinders (Maryknoll, NY: Orbis Books, 2013).

The original writings of these individuals have been changed to reflect gender inclusivity, but no other changes have been made.

To my grandchildren.

May they grow up in a world of liberty and justice for all

and share in the healing of our planet.

CONTENTS

A WORD
OF GRATITUDE

One of the great joys of my life has been the integration of pastoral ministry with writing and teaching. The reflections contained in this text emerged from a seminar I conducted titled "Homegrown Mystics," sponsored by South Congregational Church, United Church of Christ, Centerville, Massachusetts, and held from September 2018 to October 2019. I am grateful both to the seminar participants (who came from across Cape Cod) and to the congregation that supported my unique blend of scholarship and ministry. Their questions—often difficult and unfiltered—inspired my own creativity and challenged my assumptions.

I am also thankful for Ellyn Sanna's wise leadership of Anamchara Books and her faith in this project.

Finally, my wife Kate has been a companion in my scholarship, professional life, and family for over four decades, and she still inspires me to consider larger visions.

Ubuntu: "I am because of you."

1

A NATION OF MYSTICS?

The Spirit of America

Mysticism is not this or that particular cup on the table;
it is the water poured into all of them.

—VERNON HOWARD[1]

Mystics are individuals who experience God in a lively and life-transforming manner. They are, as Marcus Borg says, "spirit people," who experience the Holy moving through their lives and then share that experience with others. *God is real,* their lives proclaim; *God is alive.*

And God asks something from each of us: to be messengers of love, justice, peace,

Authentic spirituality is
revolutionary. It . . .
breaks the world; it does not
console the world, it
shatters it. And it does not
render the self content, it
renders it undone.

—KEN WILBER

and healing in the world in which we live. Mysticism is the energy that powers our message with meaning, authenticity, and sensitivity.

Mysticism begins with the solitary encounter with God deep in our souls—and then it inspires us to "go tell it on the mountain" to our families and communities. Our nation is in desperate need of this deep spirituality that flows in a constant stream from the Divine, through our inner beings, and out into the world in actions that bring justice and compassion to all who suffer oppression in any form.

A Nation in Trouble

On January 6, 2021, I watched images of people praying on bended knees, who then rose to storm the Capitol, intent on destroying sacred spaces while yelling murderous oaths. The events of that date—as much as those that occurred on 9/11—testify to the divisive nature of authoritarian and binary religious beliefs.

As I sought to understand the rage I saw on January 6, 2021, alongside the rise in race-related violence, hate crimes, and vitriol aimed at scientists and physicians, I reflected on Abraham Lincoln's first inaugural address, spoken in an earlier time of national division during which hatred and divisiveness identified with religious values and racial superiority threatened to destroy the nation:

> *Pseudo-mysticism seeks to evade reality; authentic mysticism wants to live it.*
>
> —VERNON HOWARD

We are not enemies, but friends. We must not be enemies. Though passion may have strained, it must not break our bonds of affection. The mystic chords of memory, stretching from every battle-field and patriot grave, to every living heart and hearthstone, all over this broad land, will yet swell the chorus of the Union, when again touched, as surely they will be, by the better angels of our nature.

In Lincoln's address, he invokes the spirit of mysticism. Although he doesn't define the nature of mystical experience, he points to an important aspect of the mysticism I seek to describe in this book: Mystics, who are in some way in direct contact with the Sacred, hear the chords of the moral and spiritual arcs of the universe that flow through our national life and individual lives as citizens. As mystics, we cannot fully discern God's arc of justice and healing, but we can align ourselves with God's vision for our nation, ourselves, and the world.

These days, politicians, preachers, and ordinary citizens alike speak of healing the soul of America. If the United States is to survive and flourish, the nation must reclaim a common spirit and calm the voices of hate and incivility. We must be guided by Lincoln's better angels rather than the demonic forces of our natures. The nation needs authentic repentance and transformation if it is to realize its potential to be a force for good on the planet in the perilous future that lies ahead. At this juncture in U.S. history, the American people need to open their hearts and minds to the "angelic" guidance embedded in us, as envisioned by Lincoln, a president prone to a mystical sense of Divine providence in the life of nations and people. We need to become mystics in action who join contemplation with activism and prayer with protest.

As a loyal American, I believe we as citizens need to speak out for unity, liberty, and justice for all. This is a spiritual task, taking us beyond the parochialisms of denomination, creed, political party, and even religious belief systems to affirm our essential oneness as humans and Americans. To repair the breach and heal the spirit of the United States, we need prophetic healers and activist mystics to challenge our values and show us pathways to an alternative life-supporting future. We need global citizens who recognize that planetary healing requires the interplay of spiritual critique and renewal, beginning at home before encircling the globe. We need to see the path ahead to the affirmation of religious and cultural pluralism, integrated with fidelity to our nation's highest values. Large-spirited mystics who blend spiritual commitment with concern for national well-being can lead us through the challenges of pluralism and polarization.

Mysticism is:

a. *An advanced state of inner enlightenment.*

b. *Union with Reality.*

c. *A state of genuinely satisfying success.*

d. *Insight into an entirely new world of living.*

e. *An intuitive grasp of Truth, above and beyond intellectual reasoning.*

f. *A personal experience, in which we are happy and healthy human beings.*

—VERNON HOWARD

American Mysticism

This text is my contribution to the task of healing the spirit of the United States. I have chosen, in contrast to many of my previous texts on mystical experience, to focus on mystics who identified themselves with the noblest aims of the United States while also affirming religious and cultural diversity and globalism. In this book's chapters, I describe the journey of thirteen mystics whose experience of the Holy drove them beyond self-interest to planetary loyalty, enabling them, in the words of Katherine Lee Bates, "to see beyond the years" and to intuit the horizons of what a just society might look like.

A mystic is a person who sees the facts as inadequate.

—MADELEINE L'ENGLE

These nation-shaping mystics came from various religious traditions; some were agnostics and spiritual seekers. Within their respective traditions, these thirteen American mystics each uniquely embodied a spirituality oriented toward both heavenly and earthly good. The mysticism of these individuals shows the way to a more perfect union, a democracy of spirit in which everyone matters and everyone has a voice.

These people also shaped the American experience: Although their encounters with the Holy transcend national boundaries, their spirituality was profoundly historical, embodied, and deeply rooted in their specific geographical locations. Like the Hebraic prophets, these thirteen individuals experienced the Divine as immersed in the historical process and in the affairs of politics, economics, and personal decision-making. Like Jesus, these mystics believed their spiritual visions found completion in promoting personal well-being, as reflected in the religious, political, and economic equality and freedom of all people. They challenged the accepted values of the nation, often at personal risk, and their alternative visions call us to move toward realizing the potential of the United States, while repenting the sins of slavery, racism, patriarchy, and Indigenous genocide.

Celebrating the Holy Here-and-Now, these thirteen mystics also embody a uniquely American eschatology grounded in the hope for a more perfect humanity and a national purpose that can transform the world, heralding the emergence of inclusive democracy and human flourishing. They saw that the American experiment has not yet realized the promise of equality, liberty, and justice for all. Despite denials, then and now, these mystics knew that for many people, as Langston Hughes wrote, "America was not America to me."

But these mystics imagined alternatives to the tragic realities of slavery, injustice, and poverty. Their experiences of the Holy called into question economic and political practices that prevent anyone living on U.S. soil from experiencing their spiritual destiny. They recognized that anything less than full structural and personal equality is an affront to both the democratic spirit and the Divinity whose moral and spiritual arcs inspire, energize, and critique the historical process.

Grounded in their affirmation of a democracy of revelation in which all people have equal access to Divinity, these American mystics recognized the same inalienable rights apply to all people, especially those who have been excluded from the American dream. Long before the emergence of today's liberation movements, these people's experiences of the Holy inspired them to confront structural and systemic injustice as evils contrary to the Divine plan for humanity.

As Howard Thurman asserted, "Social action, therefore, is an expression of resistance against whatever tends to, or separates one, from the experience of God, who is the ground of [the mystic's] being."[2] From Thurman's perspective and for others in this book, the mystic's encounter with the Living God inspires the quest to establish a social order in which everyone has the opportunity to experience God's fullness in their lives.

Recognizing the interdependence of life, described by Martin Luther King Jr. as a "single garment of destiny," the mystics included in this book, as well as their spiritual descendants today, challenge every social, political, and economic structure that demeans humankind and prevents humans from experiencing the Divine glory of being fully alive. They were willing to inject "good trouble" into the communities of which they were a part, in order to bring about a more perfect union and challenge the nation to go from the cramped spirit of America-first ideologies to the spaciousness of world loyalty.

Spirituality is always concrete, and American mysticism is no exception. Though we may soar to the heavens, our journey begins on the

> *Mysticism is not this or that particular cup on the table; it is the water poured into all of them.*
>
> —VERNON HOWARD

firm ground of lived experience and finds its completion in responding to the challenges of personal, national, and global realities. While there is nothing exceptional about American spirituality—each nation has its unique role to play in the unfolding of human history—our individual vocations, given to us by God, are always rooted in space and time. Mystical experiences and spiritual maturity, however, do not lead to nation-first religious nationalism. God's vision embraces every nation, inviting spiritual seekers to respect the deepest visions of all people on Earth. We can only say, "God bless America," if we are willing to also affirm the same of every other nation!

Moralism is always the cheap substitute for mysticism.

—RICHARD ROHR

The Spirit of Homegrown Mysticism

As I chart the interplay of the American experience through these thirteen mystics, I notice certain characteristics of homegrown American spirituality. These reflect the mystic's vocation to unite the local and global, the national and planetary, and the contemporary with timelessness.

Heavenly Minded for the Earthly Good

The solitary experiences of the mystics described in this book drove them to social involvement. The Holy sparked their concern for the well-being of their communities. Henry David Thoreau spoke out against the Civil War and refused to pay war taxes. Ralph Waldo Emerson went on the lecture circuit, offering an expansive vision of human destiny. Walt Whitman's delight in American diversity and the value of everyday people inspired him to become an orderly caring for the wounded during the Civil War. Maya Angelou became a national spokesperson for issues related to justice, women, and self-esteem. Black Elk offered his mystic vision as a catalyst for the renewal and healing of a struggling Indigenous community. Abraham Joshua Heschel marched with Martin Luther King Jr., and Howard Thurman, spiritual counselor to King, wrote one of the first texts on Black liberation.

These mystics were heavenly minded; they ascended into the heavens of Divine-human encounter—and then they returned to Earth to claim their vocations as God's companions in healing the world. They saw this world, in its ambiguity and tragic beauty, as the theater of Divine revelation.

The heavens declare the glory of God, but God's glory is also found in enabling all people to claim their full humanity. This asks that we challenge the injustice that stifles the human spirit. It may mean moving from the study and meditation room to the picket line or jailhouse.

Embodied Spirituality

These mystics saw Divinity in the world of the flesh. Mary Oliver knew God is as present in the lazy contemplation of a grasshopper as in a cathedral or mosque. The Earth is sacred and commands our respect and

In mysticism, knowledge cannot be separated from a certain way of life which becomes its living manifestation. To acquire mystical knowledge means to undergo a transformation.

—LOIS McMASTER BUJOLD

honor apart from human exploitation, as Black Elk and John Muir affirmed. At Christ's birth, Madeleine L'Engle wrote, the unicorn and neutrino dance for joy. The human body is a miracle, shouted Maya Angelou and Walt Whitman, and God's presence reveals itself in our sensuality and sexuality.

Bodies are sacred. Bodies—especially those wounded by racism, genocide, sexism, and homophobia—must be at the heart of our healing spirituality. A God with skin is worshipped by caring for the bodies of others, including the forgotten, abused, and oppressed. Racism, sexism, homophobia, and other structural oppressions are affronts to God's presence.

> *Love's mysteries*
> *in souls do grow,*
> *But yet the body*
> *is his book.*
>
> –JOHN DONNE

Prophetic Healing

Robert Kennedy popularized the words of George Bernard Shaw, who asserted that politics takes us from actuality to possibility: "Some [people] see things as they are, and say why? I dream of things that never were, and say why not?" The mystics described in this text imagined an alternative reality to the materialism, violence, and injustice of their time. Henry David Thoreau sojourned to the woods to find peace of mind—and there, he was inspired to social protest and civil disobedience. Abraham Joshua Heschel discovered in the biblical prophets a passionate God who challenges every form of systemic injustice, whether in the boardroom or the halls of Congress. Maya Angelou rose in self-affirmation, seeing dignity in her own painful journey as she confronted the tragic realities of American racism. John Woolman saw the inner light in enslaved people, and he wore only clothes manufactured without enslaved labor. Ann Lee and the Shakers imagined a society in which women are leaders, and ordinary work is done for heaven.

Inclusive

Mysticism also leads to globalism and inclusiveness. The democracy of revelation excludes no one, neither in the sanctuary nor the polling place. Beyond binary theologies and political stances, mystical experiences awaken us to the face of God in all things; they open us to experiencing God's presence in the human and nonhuman world. Mysticism eventually challenges every form of binary exclusivism.

Historically, mystics affirm the interdependence of all humankind. The inner light of God that John Woolman found present in himself inspired him to discover Divinity in people of all colors and to seek justice for Black and Indigenous peoples. Walt Whitman's "Song of Myself" is a hymn to the holiness of *all* people and professions, despite the uniqueness of each person, race, and profession. Maya Angelou's inaugural poem describes the planetary adventure from prehistory to the present day and concludes with the call to look your neighbor in the face and say, "Good morning." Abraham Joshua Heschel affirmed the insights of Jewish mystics who proclaimed that when you save one soul, you save the world, for in each person is a spark of Divinity. Emily Dickinson heard God's voice radiating beyond the sanctuary to the sounds of the woodlands and the conversations of companions.

Future-Oriented

Each of the thirteen mystics recognized the painful distance that lies between the American dream and the American reality. They saw the United States as a nation in formation, incomplete and often wayward yet lured forward by the quest for a more perfect union and the Divine proclamation of human equality, issuing in liberty and justice for all. As a result, a holy discontent powers American mysticism. Spirituality joins past, present, and future in a restless quest for personal and national wholeness

Mysticism joins and unites; reason divides and separates.

—THOMAS SZASZ

Mystics challenge injustice. Woolman protested slavery. Thoreau challenged wars of opportunity. Madeleine L'Engle recognized the danger of groupthink and uniformity. Black Elk imagined a new Earth in which the nation's soul is restored and the land renewed. Mystics oppose the defacing of any human being for gain or power. They yearn for a world in which the children of both the enslaved and those who enslaved walk hand in hand. They believe history leans toward justice, and eventually tyranny and slavery will fall.

As You Read This Book

In the pages ahead, as you spend time with these thirteen mystics, I invite you to see them as your contemporaries and companions. In the process, I hope you will claim your own inner mystic and outer prophet. Discover your personal and political calling to be God's companion in healing the spirit of America and the life of the planet. Be inspired to go forth into our twenty-first-century world with all its problems, buoyed up by the words of Abraham Lincoln at his second inaugural address:

> With malice toward none, with charity for all, with firmness in the right as God gives us to see the right, let us strive on to finish the work we are in, to bind up the nation's wounds, to care for him who shall have borne the battle and for his widow and his orphan, to do all which may achieve and cherish a just and lasting peace among ourselves and with all nations.

[The goal of true mysticism] is to jettison the mind-set that says "greed is good," "selfishness is normal," and "killing is necessary." Mysticism . . . is not escapism, as so many have caricatured it, but a fight for ethics and social change.

—WALTER WINK

2

RALPH WALDO EMERSON

A Bard of the Holy Ghost

*All I have seen
teaches me to trust the Creator
for all I have not seen.*

–RALPH WALDO EMERSON

"Yourself a newborn bard of the Holy Ghost, cast behind you all conformity, and acquaint men first-hand with Deity." In other words, cultivate direct experiences of God rather than relying on secondhand doctrines and rituals. So Ralph Waldo Emerson counseled the Harvard University Divinity School graduating class on July 15, 1838.

Throughout the ages, mystics have affirmed that finite humans can experience the infinite God. Eighteen hundred years before Emerson's address, the apostle Paul asserted that God's Spirit intercedes for us "with sighs too deep for words" (Romans 8:26). No sin can tarnish the realm of God within each person. The Holy Spirit is alive and speaks to us through our thoughts and the world around us. God is still speaking and shining new light on the scriptures and human experience.

In a God-filled world, the human spirit is transparent to the Holy. We live in a universe, as today's exponents of the Anthropic Principle[3] assert, that is hospitable to consciousness and mystical experiences. We can speak about Divine things because Creative Wisdom is at work in the evolutionary process and in our finite human experiences, bringing forth creatures who can contemplate and create. The Cosmic Spirit awakens us to the Infinite that gives birth to the finite. While some mystics scorn the flesh and fly from the alone to the Alone, as Plotinus counseled in the third century, other mystics, enthralled by the wonder of the universe and their own lives, experience the world as the theater of God's glory. They see human experience as a reflection of the Divine Mind undergirding and moving through all Creation.

In such a glorious universe, Emerson believed, we are challenged to engage God's revelation as mediated through our own experiences. In looking at the stars, for example, we receive a Divine gift: "the perpetual presence of the sublime."

Maltbie Babcock, a younger contemporary of Emerson's, expressed similar ideas in hymn form:

> *This is my Father's world,*
> *And to my listening ears*
> *All nature sings, and round me rings*
> *The music of the spheres.*
> *This is my Father's world:*
> *I rest me in the thought*
> *Of rocks and trees, of skies and seas;*
> *His hand the wonders wrought.*
>
> *This is my Father's world:*
> *Oh, let me ne'er forget*
> *That though the wrong seems oft so strong,*
> *God is the ruler yet.*
> *This is my Father's world,*
> *The battle is not done:*
> *Jesus who died shall be satisfied,*
> *And earth and Heav'n be one.*

In moments of mystic harmony, we see the universe as it truly is: infinite, orderly, creative, and beautiful. We recognize that despite human incivility and injustice, the moral and spiritual arcs of history will be victorious, and the more perfect union will come to pass. We feel wonder, "for the universe becomes transparent," as Emerson put it, "and higher laws than its own shine through it."

Emerson's mysticism was not passive. Reflecting the deepest harmonies of the American spirit, his form of mysticism led to mission. Contemplation inspired challenge and creativity. It empowered the battle against wrong, whether that wrong was economic exploitation, racism, or the disenfranchisement and denigration of women.

In fact, Emerson saw human experience as a laboratory for spiritual transformation. We can, Emerson counseled, trust our deepest experiences because God's Spirit undergirds our adventures in self-discovery. We know God by knowing ourselves, and in seeking God, we find ourselves. God, as an ancient saying invoked by Emerson asserts, is "a circle whose center is everywhere and whose circumference is nowhere."

> *Cultivate the habit of being grateful for every good thing that comes to you, and to give thanks continuously. And because all things have contributed to your advancement, you should include all things in your gratitude.*
>
> —RALPH WALDO EMERSON

Emerson's Life

Born in 1803, Ralph Waldo Emerson was a child of the manse, the son of a Unitarian pastor who died when Waldo, as he liked to be called, was only eight years old. As poet Mary Oliver notes in her introduction to an Emerson anthology, "Death's fast or slow lightning was a too frequent presence" throughout Emerson's life. In the wake of his father's death, the family was reduced to poverty. Yet, despite their financial straits, the family of five boys and two girls was intellectually oriented and religiously pious. As an adult, Emerson studied at Harvard University, married, and entered the ministry at Second Unitarian Church in Boston.

Tragedy struck often in his life. Three of his brothers did not make it past young adulthood, and his remaining brother had severe learning and emotional disabilities. Emerson's wife Ellen died when he was twenty-eight, plunging him into a deep depression and raising questions of faith and fate. Eventually, he came to believe that he could no longer pastor a congregation. Moreover, he doubted the significance of the Eucharist, believing it to be a spiritual commemoration rather than a required flesh-and-blood ceremony. He became convinced that "in order to be a good minister, it was necessary to leave the ministry."[4]

Needing to expand his horizons and distance himself from familiar but sorrowful environs, Emerson journeyed to Europe, where he immersed himself in the insightful literature of the day. He returned to the United States with a renewed sense of vocation: the call to share his vision of a Divinity not bound by church or sacrament but incarnate in the epiphanies of everyday life and the wonders of Nature.

God is not confined to any building, Emerson was convinced, but is the reality "in whom we live and move and have our being" (Acts 17:28). He believed the Divine Spirit addresses humanity through singing birds, babbling brooks, the crash and flash of thunder and lightning, and the roaring sea—and God speaks most fully when we listen to our deepest selves. God inspires us to self-reliance, ingenuity, and self-affirmation, all characteristics of the American ideal at its best.

Emerson was drawn to Concord, Massachusetts, approximately twenty miles from Boston (in those days, a two- or three-hour journey). Concord was emerging as a bricolage of farmers, merchants, philosophers, free thinkers, and utopian visionaries. If in the 1830s, you were to wander the countryside outside the village, you might have encountered luminaries such as Emerson and Henry David Thoreau on philosophical perambulations, engaged in a conversation with Nathaniel Hawthorne and social reformer Bronson Alcott, or seen Alcott's young daughter Louisa May (who would later write *Little Women*) at play with her sisters. Like-minded individuals gathered for erudite conversation at the Transcendentalist Club, where they debated issues of politics and morality, while putting together journals that shared a truly American philosophy.

For the remainder of his life, Emerson remained in Concord. While seldom in the pulpit after he resigned from full-time ministry, he continued to respond to people's spiritual needs as a writer, lecturer, and publisher, as well as a spiritual advisor to the emerging Transcendentalist movement. After

> *Let me never fall into the vulgar mistake of dreaming that I am persecuted whenever I am contradicted.*
>
> —RALPH WALDO EMERSON

his first wife's death, he eventually married Lydia Jackson, raised a family, and devoted himself to writing and reflecting on the presence of Divinity in flora, fauna, and human ingenuity. Although he initially struggled to make a living as a writer and lecturer, Emerson eventually became a national treasure whose work inspired common folk as well as social reformers, ministers, and philosophers.

Not content to live in the ivory tower, Emerson dreamed of an America that encouraged self-actualization among all its citizens through education and unrestricted travel. His philosophy moved from head to heart and hands, expressing itself in abolitionist activism. The soul of the universe touches everyone, he believed, and involuntary servitude stifles the sacred promise inherent in every child and adult. Like the apostle Paul, Emerson believed enlightenment could be furthered by publication and presentation. Words addressed to citizens in Concord—such as Paul's words to those in Galatia, Philippi, and Rome—could radiate across the world and the ages.

Emerson reveled in the epiphanies of everyday life and the giftedness of human potential. He saw infinity in the adventures of people and nations. As a leading figure of the American Transcendentalist movement, he perceived Divinity embodied in Nature and human experience, and he urged humankind to discover God personally and experientially rather than doctrinally or ecclesiastically.

Emerson died in 1882, from a cold that turned into pneumonia, just a month short of his seventy-ninth birthday. Newspapers referred to "Concord's irreparable loss," and the village planned a funeral that would do justice to their most important citizen. The women made black-and-white rosettes to decorate houses along the funeral procession's route, and public buildings were hung with black drapery. The railroad company arranged extra trains to bring the mourners to Concord, and workmen reinforced the floors and galleries of the church to support the weight of the throngs that flocked to mourn Emerson's loss. Louisa May Alcott brought a bouquet of jonquils to the church, and at the funeral, her father, Bronson Alcott, read a poem he had composed for the occasion.[5]

You become what you think about all day long.

—RALPH WALDO EMERSON

Nature as the Temple of God

The biblical tradition exalts God's creative wisdom in the nonhuman world. Psalm 19 proclaims:

> *The heavens are telling the glory of God;*
> *and the firmament proclaims his handiwork.*
> *Day to day pours forth speech,*
> *and night to night declares knowledge.*
> *There is no speech, nor are there words;*
> *their voice is not heard;*
> *yet their voice goes out through all the earth,*
> *and their words to the end of the world.* (verses 1–3)

Long before the emergence of Earth-denying, body-shaming theologies, this psalm affirmed a world of praise in which all things in Creation praise God. Psalm 148 sings out the same message:

> *Praise [Yahweh][6] from the earth,*
> *sea monsters and all deeps,*
> *fire and hail, snow and frost,*
> *stormy wind fulfilling his command!*

Mountains and all hills,
fruit trees and all cedars!
Wild animals and all cattle,
creeping things and flying birds! (verses 7–10)

Nature is, as the philosopher Plato proclaimed, the "moving image of eternity" and a "shrine" in which Divine Wisdom incarnates itself. Likewise, for Emerson, humankind has an original and immediate spiritual relationship with Nature. The human and the Divine are united in the natural world, and God's grandeur is present in the intestines and immune system as much as in the human spirit.

Emerson believed that by meditating on God's presence in Nature, we discover our own holiness and limitless potential to reveal God in our lives. "My own mind is the direct revelation I have from God," he wrote.

> *The lover of nature . . . has retained the spirit of infancy . . . intercourse with heaven and earth becomes part of their daily food.*
>
> —RALPH WALDO EMERSON

Standing on the bare ground—my head bathed in by the blithe air and uplifted into infinite space—all mean egotism vanishes. I become a transparent eyeball; I am nothing; I see all. The currents of Universal Being circulate through me; I am part or parcel of God. . . . I am the lover of uncontained and immortal beauty. . . . In the tranquil landscape, and especially in the distant line of the horizon, humans behold somewhat as beautiful as their own nature.

Birthed and inspired by creative Wisdom, we are made for beauty, made of beauty, and created by beauty. The beauties of Nature reflect and inspire our inner beauty. In bathing our senses in natural beauty, our interior beauty leads us to the Divine Beauty from which all things come.

According to Emerson, the universe is transparent to Divinity; it is an icon—a window—through which we see God and are led to reveal God in our own lives. Nature is the Divine incarnation that nourishes, undergirds, and inspires earthly life and mystical unity. We are one with the universe and its Creator, constantly receiving Divine wisdom and energy. Emerson asserted: "The world proceeds from the same spirit as the human body. It is a remoter and inferior incarnation of God, a projection of God in the unconscious. . . . It is therefore, to us, the present expositor of the Divine mind."

Beauty in its largest and profoundest sense, is expression for the universe. God is the all-fair. Truth, and goodness, and beauty are but different faces of the same All. But beauty in nature is not ultimate. It is the herald of inward and eternal beauty.

—RALPH WALDO EMERSON

Alienation from Nature is alienation from God and our deepest selves. Unity with the nonhuman world awakens us to the holiness of all things and inspires our own sense of Divinity and creativity.

Emerson affirmed that while doctrine, sacrament, and ritual have value, what is most important is our direct experience of the Holy. Jesus' mission was not to teach doctrines, according to Emerson, but rather, to point people to the realm of God within.

As a preacher, lecturer, and writer, Emerson believed: "It is of no use to preach to me from without. I can do that easily myself. Jesus speaks always from within, and in a way that transcends all others. In that is the miracle." Jesus is not metaphysically "other." He does not channel Divinity at the expense of humanity but reflects what it means to fully experience Divinity in human life. Jesus is the ultimate spiritual democrat, a harbinger of democracies everywhere, wanting all people to become like him in power and presence. In so doing,

Even in the mud and scum of things, something always, always sings.

–RALPH WALDO EMERSON

he becomes the model for our spiritual growth. He challenge us to awake to our own divinity. Jesus, Emerson believed, points beyond himself to the Divinity alive in all things. Jesus' message invites us to trust our prayerful experiences.

As Marcus Borg said, Jesus is a "spirit person," attentive to Divinity while radiating Divinity to others. Likewise, Emerson called on new ministers to cultivate their own experience of God, be open to God through listening, and teach congregants to go beyond secondhand religion to direct spirituality. Spiritual leadership is grounded in spiritual experience.

God is incarnate in all things, Emerson believed: "The soul is wholly embodied, and the body is wholly ensouled." Every moment in the day is an epiphany, a message from

God to individuals who awaken their senses to God's ever-present and ever-active address to humanity and all Creation.

In this view, the democracy of the spirit reflects—and requires—a democracy of values and political expression. If God touches all people, then each person must be judged as equal and entitled to equal rights. Injustice is an affront to God's ubiquitous inspiration, and the mystic must oppose it with all their heart.

While Emerson cultivated individualistic self-reliance, he also affirmed the interdependence of life: "A [person] is a bundle of relations, a knot of roots, whose flower and fruitage is the world." Even though we create our own circumstances, at the same time, the whole world conspires to create each moment of experience.

While there are many ways to encounter God within and beyond, the title of Emerson's first sermon, "Pray Without Ceasing," offers one pathway to the realm of God within our hearts. In this sermon, Emerson said that "every secret wish and every desire of the heart is a prayer."[7] Knowing that God's voice continually speaks to us, we can, with young Samuel, ask, "Speak, for your servant is listening" (1 Samuel 3:10). In listening and sensing, we discover a God-filled world and a God-filled self, which gives us everything we need to flourish and serve. As Richard Robinson notes, at the core of Emerson's life, "is

> *None of us will ever accomplish anything excellent or commanding except when we listen to this whisper which is heard by us alone.*
>
> —RALPH WALDO EMERSON

this willed surrender, this giving over to the unregarded epiphanies of every blessed day."[8]

Become a Bard of the Holy Ghost

Emerson believed that each person is a bard of the Holy Ghost. In the Spirit's democracy, each person receives Divine inspiration appropriate to their individual gifts, talents, and life experiences. God touches us with possibilities and the energy to embody them in daily life. Emerson's vision of self-reliance depends on trust in God's guidance and intimacy.

Decades ago, I was given a poster of a rainbow, inscribed with the words, "All the wonders you seek are in yourself." This statement reflects Emerson's view of human possibility: Each person's life is full of beauty and wonder, reflecting the wonder of the universe. It is appropriate to be grateful for ourselves in the same way we give thanks for the ambient universe that sustains our lives.

In ancient Celtic culture, a bard was a storyteller, poet, and singer. Like the Australian aboriginal singers, a bard charted the world with "song lines." As bards of the Spirit, we are transparent eyes, in Emerson's own poetry, who see and then sing the universe in its wonder and beauty. Bards pay attention to what their lives are saying to them—and then share these messages with the world. They can become poets of the spirit by exploring both inner and outer spaces. Awakened to beauty, they share their own unique artistry as companions of the Artist of the Universe.

In exploring your inner space, follow the example of Samuel in the Hebrew scripture: Call out to God throughout the day and then pause to be still in God's presence. Practicing the presence of God, every moment is a potential epiphany, a window into Divinity.

Take time each morning to ask for help listening to God's voice. Close your eyes and let the emotions, images, thoughts, and songs rise. While silence is good for the soul, there are times when God speaks in the many movements of our internal lives. Our inner landscape is just as revelatory of God as the outer landscape.

Recognizing that there are burning bushes everywhere, pause throughout the day to bathe your eyes in God's revelations in Nature and the nonhuman world. Notice Divinity whispering in the leaves, glistening in the babbling brook, roaring in the crashing waves, radiating in the shining sun, massaging in human touch. Each moment shines with Divinity for those who are awake and aware.

The politics of mysticism, for Emerson, emerges in the quest for a world in which every person can mine the fullness of God's Spirit within their own being and become a bard themselves, singing their own melody of joyful freedom and creativity. Our identity as bards of the Spirit challenges us to give voice to the quest for justice. To be a voice for the voiceless.

Be yourself; no base imitator of another, but your best self. There is something which you can do better than another. Listen to the inward voice and bravely obey that. Do the things at which you are great, not what you were never made for.

—RALPH WALDO EMERSON

Like Moses, our encounter with the burning bush comes with a mission—to be an agent of liberation, to share our spiritual insight with the wider society, and to support the quest for individual and community transformation.

Prayer of Awareness and Transformation

Open my eyes that I might see all the glories of Deity.
Open my heart that I might be open to graces beyond belief.
Open my senses to eternal beauty in passing time
and heavenly presence in loving touch.
Open me to God, and let me bring grace to each encounter,
inspiring beauty and justice in those around me.

3

HENRY DAVID THOREAU

The Spirit of Simplicity

Our life is frittered away by detail . . .
simplify, simplify.

–HENRY DAVID THOREAU

When I was preparing for my retirement and the move the Washington, DC, I winnowed out my books, both in my home and church. I estimated I had at least four thousand books, going back to my college days, now more than fifty years ago. Some textbooks I hadn't looked at since my first-year philosophy class at San Jose State; others were mysteries I purchased at airport bookstores as a means of escape on a coast-to-coast plane flight. The time had come to let them go.

Simplicity of life is countercultural. Our economic structure is based on consumption and ownership. We define a healthy economy in terms of money spent, products purchased, and services utilized—but our buying habits can stand between ourselves and God.

In a world where prosperity is identified with possessions, Henry David Thoreau is the apostle of simplicity. The Concord mystic sought to simplify his life so that he could focus on the business of living. One of his lifelong companions quipped that "a handful of nuts" was all Thoreau needed to be happy.[9]

Thoreau defined himself as a "mystic, a transcendentalist, and a natural philosopher to boot."[10] He cultivated what he described as the "art of seeing" and desired to strip everything that stood between him and the holiness of Nature.

The interplay of inner and outer simplicity is at the heart of Thoreau's mysticism. In simplifying our inner lives, we discover what is truly important; we come to see life as it is in all its wonder and tragedy. In simplifying our outer lives, we leave time for meditation, prayerful walking, and inspirational relationships, not to mention opportunities to be with family and loved ones. Thoreau wrote: "The order of things should be reversed, —the seventh should be humanity's day of toil . . . and the other six the Sabbath for the affections of the soul."[11]

However mean your life is, meet it and live it; do not shun it and call it hard names. . . . The fault-finder will find faults even in paradise. Love your life, poor as it is.

—HENRY DAVID THOREAU

The Life of Henry David Thoreau

Henry David Thoreau was born July 12, 1817, in Concord, Massachusetts, "the most favored spot on earth" (according to Thoreau). Although Concord was a growing village, it was surrounded by woodlands and wilderness that inspired a lifetime of sauntering.

Thoreau's father was a prosperous graphite pencil maker. (Thoreau wrote his voluminous journals and books with his father's pencils.) He sent his son to Harvard University, where Thoreau bristled against regimented studies while learning five languages.

After graduation, Thoreau returned home to become a schoolteacher, but he quit what was a lucrative position because he could not in good conscience "cane" students as a method to enforce good behavior and self-discipline. After that, Thoreau made his living as a pencil maker, handyman, principal of his own school, and surveyor.

Emerson was initially Thoreau's philosophical and professional mentor, and Thoreau was a regular resident at Emerson's Concord home, working in the gardens, doing odd jobs, and companioning Emerson's wife during his mentor's long absences as a public lecturer throughout the United States and overseas.

In 1845, at twenty-eight years of age, Thoreau decided to leave civilization and live

I learned this, at least, by my experiment: that if one advances confidently in the direction of their dreams, and endeavors to live the life which they have imagined, they will meet with a success unexpected in common hours.

–HENRY DAVID THOREAU

simply in a cabin he constructed on Walden Pond, a mile outside of Concord. Thoreau's time at Walden reflected his quest for simplicity and solitude. Living on Walden Pond allowed him to celebrate the beauty of Nature. For Thoreau, Nature was the incarnate God, a shrine to a Divinity intimately present in cycles of life and death, summer and winter, seedtime and harvest, youth and old age. Woods and weather are as revelatory as any holy scripture.

Described by a friend as a "walking muse," Thoreau exemplified *solvitur ambulando*—"it will be solved in the walking." His daily walks enabled him to directly experience the holiness of the nonhuman world. According to a neighbor, "His habit was to go abroad a portion of each day, to field or woods or the Concord River. . . . During many years he used the afternoon for walking, and usually set forth about half past two, returning at half past five."

Early on, Thoreau withdrew from the church, discovering God as much in a scudding cloud or an industrious beaver as in the liturgies and scriptures of the world's religions. Not confined to sanctuaries or scriptures, God is found everywhere—in the flowing stream, the thunder and lightning, the crashing waves,

> *I went to the woods because I wished to live deliberately, to front only the essential facts of life, and see if I could not learn what it had to teach, and not, when I came to die, discover that I had not lived.*
>
> –HENRY DAVID THOREAU

and the breaching whales—including Thoreau's own direct encounters with the Holy. In many ways, he is a forerunner

> *We need the tonic of wildness. . . . We can never have enough of nature.*
>
> —HENRY DAVID THOREAU

of today's "spiritual but not religious" movement, with its quest for holiness outside any sanctuary, scripture, sacrament, or institutional religious tradition.

Like many mystics, Thoreau's sense of Nature's sacredness was joined with his affirmation of the holiness of humankind. Mysticism leads to mission, and Thoreau's private ruminations led to political action. He embodied his commitment to the sacredness of life in his commitment to the Abolitionist movement and his participation in the Underground Railroad. During the Mexican War, he was arrested for refusing to pay his tax to support what he believed to be immoral national policies.

Thoreau charted the importance of conscientious objection in the essay "Civil Disobedience," which profoundly influenced the actions of Mahatma Gandhi in the liberation of India from British rule. He also inspired Martin Luther King Jr., and the nonviolent civil disobedience of the civil rights movement, not to mention conscientious objectors to the Vietnam War (such as myself).

> *Heaven is under our feet as well as over our heads.*
>
> —HENRY DAVID THOREAU

In *Walden*—now considered a classic reflection on the American spirit—Thoreau advocated the creation of village "commons," large woodland tracts surrounding populated areas. His writing was an inspiration for the national park system. Now more than ever, Americans need to embody Thoreau's spirit of simplicity to cultivate a sustainable economy and respond to the crisis of global climate change.

Throughout his adult life, Thoreau was plagued by chronic pulmonary ailments. In the winter of 1860, he caught a severe cold that progressed into acute tuberculosis, limiting him to indoor activities. Over the next year, his health deteriorated. When he was in a Concord jail because of his refusal to pay the taxes that supported slavery, his jailer, Sam Staples, noted that he never saw a man "dying with so much pleasure and peace." When asked by his aunt Louisa if he had peace with God, he responded, "I did not know that we had ever quarreled, Aunt." Thoreau died on May 6, 1862.

> *Let us first be as simple and well as Nature ourselves, dispel the clouds which hang over our brows, and take up a little life into our pores.*
>
> –HENRY DAVID THOREAU

In his final conversation with Thoreau, abolitionist colleague Peter Pillsbury said: "You seem so near the brink of the dark river that I almost wonder what the opposite shore may appear to you." Thoreau replied, "One world at a time."[12] His attitude reflected the spirit of the psalmist's affirmation, "This is the day that Yahweh has made. We will rejoice and be glad in it!" (Psalm 118:24 WEB). Thoreau cherished this lifetime; a meaningful and self-aware life, committed to justice and beauty, is enough. Heaven will take care of itself for those who daily saunter in the holy land.

Nature as the Mirror of Divinity

Thoreau was a Nature mystic. God spoke to him in the soaring eagle, the babbling brook, the rustling grass, and the running deer. All things are reflections of Deity, he believed, in the same way our words reflect our identity. Although Thoreau's writings seldom addressed narrowly defined religious or sectarian themes, and he did not attend church, he would have affirmed the poetry of Psalm 19:

> The heavens are telling the glory of God;
> and the firmament proclaims his handiwork.
> Day to day pours forth speech,
> and night to night declares knowledge.
> There is no speech, nor are there words;
> their voice is not heard;
> yet their voice goes out through all the earth,
> and their words to the end of the world.
> (verses 1–4)

In fact, he would have gone further than the psalmist, affirming that not only "the heavens are telling the glory of God" but that "the heavens *are* the glory of God." There is no gap between God and the world, Thoreau taught; the world is a theophany, God's encounter with us. Nature is God's word, as revelatory of Divinity as the Bible and Bhagavad Gita. Perhaps Nature is even *more* revelatory of Divinity than scripture, insofar as our experience of Nature is God revealed firsthand, while scripture is derived from other people's experiences.

Thoreau invites us to root our lives in a world of praise in which we are kin to all things. Once again, Thoreau would have felt at home in the enchanted and lively universe of the psalmist:

> Praise [Yahweh]
> Praise [Yahweh] from the heavens;
> praise him in the heights! Praise him, all his angels;
> praise him, all his host!
> Praise him, sun and moon;
> praise him, all you shining stars!
> Praise him, you highest heavens,
> and you waters above the heavens!
> Let them praise the name of [Yahweh],
> for he commanded and they were created.
> He established them forever and ever;
> he fixed their bounds, which cannot be passed.
> Praise [Yahweh] from the earth, you sea monsters
> and all deeps, fire and hail, snow and frost,
> stormy wind fulfilling his command!
> Mountains and all hills, fruit trees and all cedars!
> Wild animals and all cattle,
> creeping things and flying birds!
> (Psalm 148:1–10)

The world is the theatre of Divine beauty, and Nature's praise is always full-bodied and full-throated.

Thoreau's detailed sketches of natural phenomena are not purely observational and scientific; they are revelational.

God is not separate from the world. Instead, the Spirit is moving in and through the world.

Scholars debate whether Thoreau was a pantheist, identifying God and the world as one seamless reality, or if he was what today is called a panentheist, viewing the world as infused by a Divinity who is yet more than the world, in the same way that intelligence is present throughout the body—our cells, organs, and systems—and not restricted to the mind and brain. For Thoreau, everything in life and death mirrors Divinity.

> *An early-morning walk is a blessing for the whole day.*
>
> —HENRY DAVID THOREAU

In so doing, his approach is like that of Saint Francis, whose "Canticle of the Sun" describes not only the sun and moon and Nature as our siblings but also death as our brother and friend.

Similar in spirit to Saint Francis, Thoreau saw Divinity wherever he saw matter of any kind. When it came to humanity, he believed we are not an alien species, separated from Nature but rather, we partake of Nature. The stars are our distant relations and "all material things are in some sense humanity's kindred, and subject to the same laws."[13] In contrast to the emerging materialism of the nineteenth century—and the consumerism of the twenty-first century with its chants of "drill, baby, drill"—Thoreau affirmed an enchanted reality in which physical matter and the invisible spirit world are so connected that they are virtually one.

A Spirituality of the Senses

Thoreau identified himself as a mystic, but his mysticism was one of immersion in the world of the senses, not an escape from the flesh-and-blood world of embodiment and Nature. While some mystics see embodiment—both the human body and the nonhuman world—as a prison house and an impediment to spiritual growth, Thoreau believed we find God best in the world of the senses. "If God is anywhere, then God is everywhere."[14] As the Gospel of Thomas asserts, "Cleave the wood and I [the Christ] am there" (77). If the monk is all eye, as a Desert Father once said, Thoreau would go still further: The mystic is all sensory experience.

I believe that there is a subtle magnetism in Nature, which, if we unconsciously yield to it, will direct us aright.

—HENRY DAVID THOREAU

The inner world of spirit is congruent with the outer world of Nature, reflecting the Divinity of both. "This is a delicious evening," wrote Thoreau, "when the whole body is one sense, and imbibes delight through every pore. I go and come with a strange liberty in nature, a part of herself." Every moment leans into infinity for those whose senses are open.

Thoreau was a mystic of place, and his sacred place was Concord. But the "thin place" of Concord, translucent to Divinity, is everywhere, confronting us with each sight and step.

Thoreau was saddened to see people "blind to a beauty that is beaming on every side of them."[15] We need to train our senses to the experience of beauty. When we open the doors of perception, Nature reveals Divinity in every leaf and sunset. In Thoreau's words, an individual "flows at once to God when the channel of purity is open." We experience oneness with the nonhuman world when we "still the mind, open the body, clear the senses" through a process of deep listening that encompasses every sense.

Far from being impediments to the spiritual life, the senses are avenues to Divinity. The world of Nature does not point to a greater reality; it *is* the Greater Reality, a revealing of God as true as the world of ideas. Eternity is found in the dynamic movements of Nature and our own lives. As Thoreau asserted, "The life of a wise person is most of all extemporaneous, for they live out of an eternity that includes all time."[16]

Thoreau concludes *Walden* with a hymn to Divine light radiating in all things. "Only that day dawns in which we are awake. There is more day to dawn. The sun is but a morning star." Divinity is the spirit of the world, and the world is the body of God.

Mysticism and Prophetic Critique

Mysticism embeds us in the world. Although Thoreau retreated from the world of consumerism, seeking the simplicity that enables us to see Divinity in all things and breaks down the barriers between humanity and holiness, at the same time, his retreat inspired his immersion in the harsh realities of injustice. "Could a greater miracle take place than for us to look through each other's eyes for an instant?" Thoreau asks as he ponders diversity at the cosmic and human levels.[17]

This sense of holiness inspired Thoreau and his family to provide clandestine comfort to those headed to freedom in Canada on the Underground Railroad. He identified with the hopelessness and suffering of America's slaves. According to Laura Dassow Walls, his "deep empathy also opened Thoreau up radically to the world. Injustice to another made him storm with the passionate and sleepless rage that powered his great writings of political protest."[18]

Thoreau could not venture forth on his daily walks without being confronted by the hell that was the everyday experience of slaves. In looking at a nation still supporting slavery, Thoreau confessed to a deep and soul-shattering grief: "At last it occurred to me that what I lost was a country."[19] Empathy deepens both our joy and pain, allowing us to hear the cries of the oppressed. "I walk toward one of our ponds," Thoreau wrote, "but what signifies the beauty of nature when men are base? . . . The remembrance of my country spoils my walk."[20]

> *If I have unjustly wrested a plank from a drowning man, I must restore it to him though I drown myself.*
>
> —HENRY DAVID THOREAU

Throughout his life, Thoreau saw holiness in humanity, and that vision led him to protest anything that stood in the way of a person experiencing Divine glory. As the lives of other, more modern mystics—such as Howard Thurman, Thomas Merton, and Dorothy Day—reveal, our experiences of holiness call us to make our world safe for every human soul. The encounter with God challenges us to confront every form of racism and systemic injustice, most particularly state-sanctioned forms of injustice and dehumanization. The democracy of Divine Presence requires expanding the circle of justice to include everyone.

Holy Sauntering

For Thoreau, the art of seeing was connected with the art of walking. In his classic text on walking, Thoreau wrote that "I have met with but one or two people in the course of my life who understood the art of Walking, that is, of taking walks—who had a genius so to speak for SAUNTERING."[21] The word "sauntering" is derived from descriptions of pilgrims on their way to the Holy Land, *le Sante Terre*. As they walked by, Thoreau speculated, children shouted, "There goes a Sante-Terre, a Saunterer, a Holy Lander."[22]

Thoreau confessed, "I think that I cannot preserve my health and spirits, unless I spend four hours a day at least—and it is commonly more than that—sauntering through the woods and over the hills and fields, absolutely free from all worldly engagements."[23] On his walks, Thoreau said, "I enter a swamp as a sacred place, —a sanctum sanctorum."[24] In walking we

It is something to be able to paint a particular picture, or to carve a statue, and so to make a few objects beautiful; but it is far more glorious to carve and paint the very atmosphere and medium through which we look, which morally we can do. To affect the quality of the day, that is the highest of arts.

—HENRY DAVID THOREAU

experience "a newer testament, —the gospel according to this moment."[25]

Walking is essential to my own spiritual journey. For many years, virtually every morning—sun, rain, or snow—I walked the beaches of Cape Cod near my home. After moving to the Washington, DC, suburbs, I now walk tree-lined streets and on the Potomac shores as sunrise bathes the beauty of lush woodlands. Some days, my walks are punctuated by focused prayerful affirmations and intercessions. Other days, I am simply "all sense," bathing my eyes in sun, surf, sand, and sky—or tree and river—with no particular intent, rejoicing in the amazing cavalcade of the holy here-and-now. Many mornings, the deer are my only companions. Over the years, I have also gone on "preaching walks," not preaching at others, but letting wisdom scripture percolate as I saunter through my neighborhood. Insights and inspirations bubble up as I "wonder as I wander."

I invite you to also become a Saunterer, a walker in the holy land of your neighborhood, whether it be on a seashore, a city street, a woodland, or a suburban neighborhood. Now that I have retired to the Washington, DC, suburbs, I claim the holy land of Bethesda's streets, the cobblestones of Georgetown, the Potomac towpath, and the quiet trails just a mile from my home. I revel in early morning strolls on the Capitol Mall, as I listen to the heartbeat of the nation and pray for the healing of our national spirit.

There are no prerequisites to walking prayers and meditations. Simply open your spirit to Divinity with every step. You may choose to focus on your breath or a prayer word;

you might pray for a particular problem or intercede on behalf of a friend, family member, or a situation in the larger community, nation, or world. You may also open yourself to the "sacrament of the present moment" (as described in the eighteenth century by mystic Pierre de Caussade) while you rejoice in the constantly changing panorama of Nature. Open your senses to your environment, noticing the wonder of each moment and every place. If you are so inclined, say "thank you," to the Wisdom-Within-Nature. Rejoice with Thoreau:

> So we saunter toward the Holy Land, till one day the sun shall shine more brightly than it has ever done, shall perchance shine into our minds and hearts, and light up our whole lives with a great awakening light, as warm and serene and golden as on a bankside in autumn.[26]

Prayer of Awareness and Transformation

With every step, let me walk in beauty.
Fill me with wonder and amazement at Life.
Inspire me to love the Earth
and protect its beauty.

4

WALT WHITMAN

A Democracy of Revelation

Without enough wilderness America will change.
Democracy, with its myriad personalities
and increasing sophistication,
must be fibred and vitalized by regular contact
with outdoor growths—animals, trees,
sun warmth and free skies—or it will dwindle and pale.

—WALT WHITMAN

Traditional theology speaks of God as omnipresent, omniscient, and omnipotent; that is, God is present everywhere and in all things; aware of everything that occurs from the outside in and the inside out; and providentially active in all Creation, large and small. While these concepts are variously understood by theologians, from a mystical and poetic viewpoint they serve to inspire wonder and amazement at God's unique relationship with all Creation. God is, as the apostle Paul asserts, quoting the wisdom of the Greeks, the Reality "in whom we live and move and have our being" (Acts 17:28). The Infinite is also the Intimate. Wherever we are, God is present working providentially and lovingly in our lives, knowing and responding to our deepest needs, and providing guidance appropriate to every occasion. God's active presence in all things does not eliminate creaturely freedom and creativity but undergirds our agency and responsibility. When we reach the end of our powers, however, God comes to our aid, providing a way where we perceive no way.

Divine omnipresence is at the heart of God's nature, according to virtually every Christian and Jewish theologian. God is not solely out there, as the Deists asserted, acting at the beginning to set up the laws of Nature and then moving to the sidelines as an observer or an occasional miracle worker. Divine omnipresence means that God's providential care is moving in our lives and all Creation, every millisecond and in each encounter. All things reveal something of God and are manifestations, to a greater or lesser degree, of Divine wisdom, albeit often opaquely. The heavens declare the glory of God and so do our reproductive and digestive systems in all their wondrous earthiness. God aims at wholeness in all things, at

Not I nor anyone else can travel that road for you. You must travel it by yourself. It is not far. It is within reach. Perhaps you have been on it since you were born, and did not know. Perhaps it is everywhere—on water and land.

—WALT WHITMAN

liberty and justice for all, and wants us to be companions in achieving the Divine vision of "on earth as it is in heaven."

No poet or mystic more fully reveled in God's presence in the commonplace, earthy, and embodied aspects of the world than Walt Whitman, who saw himself as the poet of soul and body, both of which radiate Divine glory. Whitman self-identified as the bard and sage of the commonplace, what he described as "the divine average," embodied in our cells and souls, and in the emerging American democracy. Like Plato, Whitman saw the nation as the soul written large, its amazing diversity and dynamism revealing the providential movements of God.

A lover of the United States and a patriot with few peers in the literary world, Whitman believed the ebb and flow of our national unfolding revealed the movements of Divine wisdom. Not imprisoned by the small-minded bloviations of "nation-first" politicians, whose nationalism is characterized by bellicose rhetoric and privileging of the wealthy and powerful, Whitman saw God's revelation in the nation's spirit as a light to the world and a call to authentic democracy that treasures the gifts, experience, and values of each person, regardless of race, ethnicity, gender, sexuality, or occupation.

God numbers the hairs on our heads—and in Whitman's earthy words, the scent of our armpits "is aroma finer than prayer." God also inspires the arc of national life as it bends toward justice and freedom. Our daily occupations awaken us to the interdependence of life and the holiness of good work. Appearances notwithstanding, God's creativity flows onward within the historical process. Hallelujah! God's truth is marching on!

Whitman's Life

Born on Long Island in 1819, the son of a speculative and mostly unsuccessful builder (what today we would call a house "flipper"), Walt Whitman grew up in Brooklyn, New York. As a result of his father's business failures, the family was always on the edge of poverty. At age twelve, Whitman went to work as an apprentice printer, orienting his professional focus toward journalism and publishing.

In his late teens and throughout his twenties, the precocious Whitman became a reporter and then an editor of several newspapers. During this time, he discovered his vocation as a poet who celebrated the holiness of human experience as revealed in the body electric and in the emerging and conflicted nation.

Although Whitman was intellectually gifted, he was drawn to the common person, the rough and hardscrabble tradesperson, coach driver, and

> *Happiness, not in another place but this place . . . not for another hour, but this hour.*
>
> —WALT WHITMAN

farmer. Nothing was foreign to this celebrant of the "divine average," the imprint of God in everyday people as well as the great people of history. Divine revelation is broadcast generously throughout Creation and humankind, and Whitman embraced generous embodiments of Divinity in his song of himself—ultimately the song of everyone—and his aspiration to be America's greatest poet.

The reading public saw Whitman's poetry as both genius and immoral. While tame by today's standards, Whitman's celebration of embodiment and sexuality as avenues to Divinity scandalized many of his nineteenth-century readers and literary critics. Nevertheless, Whitman's *Leaves of Grass* transformed American poetry, liberating it from the straitjacket of tradition, and awakening readers to the holiness of life's every day, embodied, and ensouled experiences. Whitman sought to love God in the world of the flesh, all flesh—the beautiful and the grotesque—and to promote a democracy of revelation in which everyone, not just pastors and theologians, experience the dynamic, electric movements of God. Bodies, spirits, and national life reveal the miraculous nature of ordinary reality and inspire what Abraham Joshua Heschel described as radical amazement.

> *I like the scientific spirit —the holding off, the being sure but not too sure, the willingness to surrender ideas when the evidence is against them: this is ultimately fine—it always keeps the way beyond open—always gives life, thought, affection, the whole person, a chance to try over again.*
>
> —WALT WHITMAN

During the Civil War, Whitman worked as a wound dresser, first, in New York and later in Washington, DC. As a companion to the wounded and dying, Whitman found solidarity with suffering humankind. Deeply empathetic, he experienced the pain of those he served as his own pain. There is no "other," he discovered; our joys and sorrows are one. Large-souled people embrace life's dynamic interconnection that joins us in celebration and grief. Whitman wrote: "I never before had my feeling so thoroughly and (so far) permanently absorbed, to the very roots, as by these huge swarms of dear, wounded, sick, dying boys."[27] Colonel Richard Hinton described Whitman's mission to the wounded soldiers:

> A wounded soldier don't like to be reminded of his God more than twenty times a day. . . . Walt Whitman didn't bring any tracts or Bibles; he didn't ask if you loved the Lord, and didn't seem to care whether you did or not . . . this old heathen came and gave me a pipe and tobacco . . . about the most joyous moment of my life.[28]

Whitman's vision of the divine average incarnates what Therese of Lisieux described as ordinary acts done with great love. The hungry, thirsty, abandoned, and vulnerable don't need doctrine; they first need love and respect.

Whitman's unorthodox mysticism, joining body and spirit as equal revelations of Divinity, and imperfectly embodied in his own personal struggles and quest for fame, led him to see holiness in the wounded and dying as well as the enslaved people the Union soldiers sought to free. Mysticism is about vision, about seeing more than meets the eye, and discovering beauty hidden by the violence and injustice of the world.

I see behind each mask that wonder—a kindred soul.

–WALT WHITMAN

Whitman's mysticism is complex and runs counter to our typical understanding of spirituality. He believed the sensual reveals Divinity as much as the world's scriptures.

God spoke to Jesus and the Hebraic sages—and God also inspired the authors of the Hindu spiritual classic, the *Bhagavad Gita*. God inspired the love poems of the Song of Solomon and the spiritual and relational ecstasy of Rumi. Whitman was ambitious and sought fame, but his quest was guided by his profound encounters with Divinity in his own flesh and blood, in the bodies of others, and in the holiness of the nonhuman world.

After the Civil War, Whitman worked several years as a civil servant in Washington, DC, joining governmental service with poetry and ministry to wounded veterans. In 1873, the previously robust Whitman suffered a stroke, which left him partially paralyzed and forced him to move to Camden, New Jersey, where he lived with his brother for the remainder of his life. Meanwhile, his reputation as the nation's poet continued to grow, even though *Leaves of Grass* was temporarily withdrawn from publication due to being deemed obscene. Whitman died in 1892, just short of his seventy-second birthday.

You Are a Temple of God

Walt Whitman celebrated body and soul, flesh and spirit, as revelations of God. The democracy of the spirit also embraces the affirmation of the flesh.

Mystical experiences can occur during times of solitary meditation. They can also occur as we gaze at the sunset, observe the city waking up and people going to work, minister to the wounded and dying, and share expressions of intimacy with loved ones. The doctrine of omnipresence means

God is everywhere, moving through every act, inspiring us to experience Divinity in all things. Omnipresence inspires a spiritual vision that is holistic, not dualistic or polarizing. Accordingly, our bodies can be as legitimate expressions of Divinity as our spirits. The apostle Paul captures a similar holy embodiment:

> *Do you not know that your body is a temple of the Holy Spirit within you, which you have from God, and that you are not your own? For you were bought with a price; therefore glorify God in your body.* (1 Corinthians 6:16)

Paul challenges us to glorify God in our bodies, for they are shrines of Divinity. In Paul's Letter to the Corinthians, he speaks against promiscuous and exploitive sexual behaviors, but he does not condemn sexuality as a whole and says nothing to criticize healthy and loving sexual relationships.

> *This is what you should do: love the earth and sun and the animals, despise riches, give alms to everyone that asks, stand up for the stupid and crazy, devote your income and labor to others hate tyrants, argue not concerning God, have patience and indulgence toward the people, . . . re-examine all you have been told at school or church or in any book, dismiss what insults your own soul, and your very flesh shall be a great poem.*
>
> —WALT WHITMAN

Glorifying God in embodiment means caring for our own bodies and the bodies of others in a holy and joyful way. In that spirit, Whitman believed the body is inspired and the spirit embodied:

> *Behold the body includes, and is the meaning,*
> *the main concern . . . of the soul.*
> *Whoever you are, how superb and how divine*
> *is your body, or any part of it.*

In the spirit of the Genesis creation story, which pronounces all Creation, human and nonhuman, as good, Whitman affirmed "the flesh and appetites. Seeing, hearing, feeling, are miracles, and each part and tag of me is a miracle." While Whitman's spirituality scandalized body-denying spiritual practitioners and puritans, his sense of God's presence in everything, from physical pleasure to a dung heap, made him see the entire world as filled with icons and pathways to holiness.

> *To me, every hour*
> *of the day and night*
> *is an unspeakably perfect miracle.*

We are wondrously made and reveal holiness as we go to work, play with our children, or enjoy intimacy with our lovers. The complexity of life is to be embraced, not scorned. In growing in wisdom and stature, we recognize that we are multiplicity, a "cosmos" containing joy and sorrow, good and evil, contemplation and passion. Spiritual maturity is found in embracing rather than denying the complexities of life.

The omnipresent God is at work in the light and dark, love and hate, and life and death. Creation reflects a democracy of experience, and its personal and global diversity reflects the movements of a pluralistic God. Within our personal "multitude," as Whitman described himself, or the diversity of the universe, the structure and guiding star of the Creation is love. Love truly makes the world go round, and love parents a world where Divinity can be found as fully in our personal struggles and passions as in religious contemplations or holy sacraments.

All Is Miracle

Whitman experienced the universe, large and small, as an enchanted reality. Life bursts forth in buzzing honeybees and the birth of a child. Holiness and wonder come to us while we walk Manhattan's busy streets or as we witness a sunrise.

> *I believe a leaf of grass*
> *is no less than the journey-work of the stars,*
> *And the pismire is equally perfect . . .*
> *And a mouse is miracle enough to stagger*
> *sextillions of infidels.*

Blades of grass . . . ants and bees . . . scurrying rodents: Existence is miraculous. Think of the complex and interdependent processes, involving billions of cells and neurons, that are occurring as you read this book. Ponder the amazing reality of conception, gestation, and birth, whether of a gnat, whale, or human child. Contemplate the wondrous beauty of photographs from the Hubble telescope, now revealing a trillion galaxies and two hundred sextillion suns like our own, with more to come. Rejoice in a starry, starry night or a child cuddling with you at bedtime. Radical amazement is surely in order when we ponder the grandeur of the universe and the complexity of the infinitesimal. The intimate and the microscopic are equally as marvelous as the mighty and immense.

There is no need for supernatural revelation or infallible scriptures. The universe is the primary word of God. All places can become, as the Celts averred, "thin places," where Heaven and Earth, Divinity and embodiment, meet and unite in the love song of the universe. And so, Whitman exclaims, "O amazement of things—even the least particle! O spirituality of things."

For every atom belonging to me as good belongs to you.

—WALT WHITMAN

Radical Empathy

Whitman's universe is dynamic, complex, interdependent, and God-filled. The poet-mystic wrote: "I hear and behold God in every object."

In the gentle and sometimes turbulent providence of God, life unites us, similar to the body of Christ Paul described: "If one member suffers, all suffer together with it; if one member is honored, all rejoice together with it" (1 Corinthians 12:27). The complex and pluralistic self that Whitman embraced is intimately related to every other self.

No ultimate boundary exists between the individual and the universe, your experience and mine. Your pain is mine and so is your joy.

Whitman confessed, "I do not ask the wounded person how he feels, I myself become the wounded person." Moreover, in the intricate interdependence of life, "Whoever degrades another, degrades me." Whitman charted a spirituality and politics of empathy in which there is no "other," and we are all joined by the "mystic chords" of memory and hope.

A century later, Vietnamese monk Thich Naht Hanh spoke of this same joyful-painful interdependence of life, which breaks down the barriers between self and other.

> I am the frog swimming happily in the clear pond,
> and I am also the grass-snake who . . .
> feeds itself on the frog.
> I am the child in Uganda, . . .
> my legs as thin as bamboo sticks,
> and I am the arms merchant,
> selling deadly weapons to Uganda.
> I am the twelve-year-old girl . . .
> who throws herself into the ocean
> after being raped by a sea pirate,
> and I am the pirate, my heart not yet capable
> of seeing and loving.[29]

There is no other; nothing is separate from myself. All of us are one in body and spirit, soul and marrow, activity and receptivity. The outer and the inner join as we become what we see. For people whose senses are open, the other becomes their deepest self. "There was a child went forth every day," wrote Whitman. "And the first object he looked upon that object he became." God is "immanent in every life and object," and so are we. We are one in the tragic beauty of all Creation. In that sense of unity, wherever we are, we are home.

Loving God in the World of the Flesh

Walt Whitman described himself both as the poet of the body and the poet of the soul. Body and soul are not two different realities but interpenetrate each other. Divine omnipresence ensures that body and spirit alike are windows into revelation, avenues to experience the Divine. God is embedded in the cells of our bodies, the beating of our hearts, and our feelings of pleasure as well as pain. Divine love is reflected in lovers' embraces, as the Song of Songs proclaims. The beauties of the Earth do not merely point to a distant and unchanging Beauty but are beautiful in and of themselves; we can, with W. H. Auden, "love God in the world of the flesh."[30]

Tragically, however, many of us disparage our bodies. We feel shame when we look in the mirror. We compare ourselves to the "heavenly bodies" of models, actors, and actresses. We fear aging and see the appearance of wrinkles as diminishment that must be hidden by cosmetics and surgery. And yet, as temples of the Spirit, our bodies are divinely and wondrously fashioned. The workings of our immune system, the firings of neurons, the processes of seeing and hearing are miraculous. Whatever our current health, we are amazing, a wonder to behold in pain and joy.

Just as tragically, we disparage the bodies of others through our cultural judgments of beauty and ugliness. We fail to ensure that every child has an adequate diet and safe place to live. Loving God in the world of the flesh may mean simplifying our lives and changing our diets so that others may experience the abundance we take for granted. Body spirituality reminds us of the holiness of every body and the respect each body deserves. Body spirituality leads to body politics.

My body makes my immortal experience.

—WALT WHITMAN

In this next spiritual practice, I invite you to begin with an Examen of the Body.[31] You may choose to look in a mirror or scan your unclothed body. Take time to notice your embodiment—your appearance, the feel of your skin, your overall well-being. How do you feel about your body? What gives you pleasure? What gives you pain? How would you describe your current health?

What is the most joyous experience of embodiment you have? It need not be spectacular by the world's standards. A ninety-year-old I know rejoices in his ability to drive to the beach where he meditates on the sea, sky, and sand each morning. Sitting in his beach chair, he experiences the pleasures of sight and sound. On a hot day, the feel of cold water flowing down your throat can be a great delight. For lovers, the joy of physical and spiritual union and the delight, even after a long marriage, of a loving touch allow us to revel in the pleasures our bodies offer us.

In the film *Chariots of Fire*, Olympic runner Eric Liddell delights in his embodiment and feels the synchronicity of Divine and human pleasure: "I believe that God made me for a purpose. But He also made me fast, and when I run, I feel His pleasure." Where do you experience God's pleasure?

Take time to reflect on joyful embodiment. Where do you experience God's pleasure in physical activity? In my own Examen, I recognized that I feel God's pleasure when I write and teach, walk and read with my grandchildren, enjoy natural beauty, go to bed each night with my life companion beside me, and then wake up before sunrise to a day full of possibility.

The spirit receives from the body just as much as it gives to the body, if not more.

—WALT WHITMAN

As part of your spiritual disciplines, commit yourself to practices that give you healthy pleasure. It may not be running, yoga, or Pilates; it could be something gentler. In my case, it is a long walk on the beach, gazing at the place where sea, sky, and sand are joined. It may also be a walk in an arboreal suburban neighborhood or on a park trail. I also delight in a well-cooked healthy meal, as well as the hand of a grandchild tucked in my own or the closeness I feel as my wife and I lie together in bed, reading, watching television, or enjoying each other's companionship.

Let your embodiment be a prayer. Give thanks for physical joy. If you have bodily and health changes, pray to see yourself in a new light. If necessary, seek the assistance of a compassionate counselor or physical health consultant.

Finally, as you commit yourself to loving your own body, explore the ethics of embodiment. Seek justice for the bodies of others: give generously to the local food bank, support legislation that ensures every child receives an adequate diet, become part of a group such as Bread for the World that advocates for a national response to global malnutrition. Learn about human slavery and trafficking. Challenge racist behaviors and police practices that put LGBTQ+, brown, and Black bodies at risk. Be aware that sex trafficking and other forms of servitude may be occurring even in your hometown.

Rejoice in your breath, in the feel of your skin, in the senses—and give thanks by your concern for the well-being of others.

Prayer of Awareness and Transformation

God of all Creation,
who comes to us embodied in a little child,
who delights in the senses, and creates all things good,
help me to love your Creation, your embodiment,
in my own body and in the bodies of others.
Let me treat every body, every person, with respect.
Let me honor the bodies of others,
ethically and relationally.
And let me give thanks
for the wonder of my being and all Creation.

5

EMILY DICKINSON

Spirituality Without Certainty

After a great pain, a formal feeling comes—
The stiff Heart questions. . . .
—then the letting go—

—EMILY DICKINSON

Celtic Christians describe certain places as "thin places," where humankind and Divinity meet and where earthly life becomes a medium of Divine revelation—and I believe that the same applies to people. Certain people seem to be transparent to Divinity. This is not always as the result of deep spiritual practices or moral commitments; they seem to simply dwell in a Divine atmosphere, touched by God's presence despite all their imperfections, doubts, and failures.

One of the great figures of biblical spirituality is Jacob, the patriarch, trickster, and wrestler with God. Apart from Jesus, Moses, Mary, and the apostle Paul, no biblical figure's spiritual journey reflects the drama of encountering God with greater intimacy and intensity than the morally ambiguous and spiritually sensitive Jacob.

Jacob's spiritual journey begins with a dream. Fleeing the wrath of his brother Esau, from whom he's cheated their father Isaac's blessing and birthright, Jacob spends the night on the outskirts of Luz. With just a stone for a pillow, he has an amazing dream, in which he perceives a ladder of angels ascending from Earth to heaven and back again. He also receives the promise of Divine companionship and blessing. When he awakens, terrified and awestruck, he stammers, "Surely [Yahweh] was in this place—and I did not know it! . . . How awesome is this place! This is none other than the house of God, and this is the gate of heaven" (Genesis 28:16-17).

> *Dwell in possibility.*
> *Find ecstasy in life; the*
> *mere sense of living is*
> *joy enough.*
>
> —EMILY DICKINSON

Years later, on the verge of meeting his brother Esau and fearful that the brother he cheated years before might seek revenge, Jacob rests in another solitary place, near the stream of Jabbok, where he wrestles all night with a stranger (Genesis 32:22-32). As morning dawns, the stranger seeks to end the contest. Despite his injury, Jacob persists and demands, "I will not let you go, unless you bless me." Although Jacob never receives the stranger's name, surely the stranger is the Holy One. Jacob receives a blessing and a new name, Israel, "for you," the angel tells him, "have striven with God and humans and have prevailed." Limping into the pulse of a new morning, Jacob exclaims, "For I have seen God face to face, and yet my life is preserved."

Jacob's life-and-death struggle with the great and inscrutable Mystery was the heart of Emily Dickinson's spiritual vision. Still short of thirty and just beginning to claim her vocation as a poet, Dickinson wrote:

> A little East of Jordan,
> Evangelists record,
> A Gymnast and an Angel
> Did wrestle long and hard
> Till morning touching mountain—
> And Jacob, waxing strong,
> The Angel begged permission
> To Breakfast—to return—
> Not so, said cunning Jacob!
> "I will not let thee go
> Except thou bless me"—Stranger!
> The which acceded to—
> Light swung the silver fleeces
> "Peniel" Hills beyond,
> And the bewildered Gymnast
> Found he had worsted God! (Poem 59)

Jacob's encounters with God exemplify the mysticism of the numinous, described by German theologian and philosopher Rudolf Otto (1869–1937). In his classic, *The Idea of the Holy*, Otto describes mystical experiences—encounters with the Holy—in terms of mystery, terror, fascination, and grace. The Divine, by whatever name we call it, is the "wholly other," beyond any concept or description, the dazzling darkness or dark energy, from which each creature emerges. The Holy is awesome—awe-full—and its grandeur and power provokes Jacob's terror.

In power and presence, the Divine is fascinating and alluring. With the hymn writer, we can proclaim "How Great Thou Art," as we reflect on "all the worlds Thy hands have made," as we view photos from the Hubble telescope or read of the immense and intricate universe journey from the Big Bang to the twenty-first century. When we view our infinitesimal place in the universe, we can stammer with the author of Psalm 8: "What are humans that you are mindful of them, mortals that you care for them?" Yet, the Infinite takes shape in intimate encounters, addressing us personally and uniquely. In moments of insight, we may discover the human face of Divinity in a child born in a manger who suffers for our salvation or a spiritual seeker sitting under the Bo Tree.

Centuries later, Emily Dickinson embodied in the life of a pugilist and poet, as she described herself, this same awe and wonder, terror and doubt, that characterized Jacob's experience of the Holy. Believing her-

To live is so startling it leaves little time for anything else.

-—EMILY DICKINSON

self to be called to be a poet, just as Jesus was called to be a proclaimer of justice, Dickinson saw her poetry as a dialogue with God and a window on the wondrous handiwork of Divine creativity.

Recently, I came upon a T-shirt that quoted Emily Dickinson: "I'm nobody! Who are you?" This line from one of her poems could describe the nineteenth-century poet, who spent much of her life in seclusion, seldom left Amherst, Massachusetts, and allowed only eleven of her 1,775 poems to be published in her lifetime. The entire poem reflects not only her anonymity but the infinitesimal nature of creaturely life in a mysterious, awesome, and God-filled world.

> I'm Nobody! Who are you?
> Are you—Nobody—too?
> Then there's a pair of us!
> Don't tell! they'd advertise—you know!
> How dreary—to be—Somebody!
> How public—like a Frog—
> To tell one's name—the livelong June—
> To an admiring Bog! (Poem 288)

The Life of Emily Dickinson

Self-described as a "runaway nun" and known as the "great recluse" among the citizens of Amherst, Massachusetts, Emily Dickinson lived in a God-haunted world. She was born in 1830, the daughter of a lawyer and politician who was one of the leaders in the establishment and advancement of Amherst College. One of her biographers notes that "the only truly remarkable thing about Emily Dickinson's existence is that she produced a great deal of remarkable poetry."[32] Yet, from the vantage point of her corner bedroom at the family homestead in Amherst, working at her diminutive writing desk. she surveyed the universe and wrestled with its Creator.

In the wake of the Great Awakening and the impact of the theological preaching of Jonathan Edwards, the young people of Western Massachusetts were expected to accept traditional Christianity. During her year at Mount Holyoke Women's Seminary (now Mount Holyoke College), Dickinson was regularly subjected to sermons on the themes of salvation and the second coming to Christ, but try as she might, she could not accept the call to come to Christ. She remained one for which, in the language of the day, there was "no hope."

In this "come to Jesus," soul-saving revival environment, Dickinson's problem was not Jesus, whom she described as the "tender pioneer." She objected to the idea of an omnipotent and inscrutable Godhead. She felt great admiration for the "tender pioneer" and experienced a sense of holiness and wonder at Divine creativity incarnate in Nature and human passion, but she struggled, like Jacob, with finding a God whose character she could trust and affirm. In reflecting on an experience of her youth, she gave thanks for the words of a preacher who showed her a different vision of God. "I shall never forget the Doctor's prayer, that first morning with you—so simple, so believing—*That* God must be a friend—*that* was a different God—and I almost felt warmer myself, in the midst of a tie so sunshiny."[33] Like

> *The soul should always stand ajar, ready to welcome the ecstatic experience.*
>
> —EMILY DICKINSON

many of today's self-described "spiritual but not religious" pilgrims, Dickinson's life was spirit-centered but not doctrinal or institutional in orientation.

She found the God of Calvinism and the evangelical preachers to be intellectually troubling and existentially frightening. On the one hand, preachers proclaimed the embodiment of God's love in the gentle Galilean, who beckoned the children to come to him. On the other hand, the God proclaimed by the Calvinist tradition was also all-powerful, often destructive and wrathful, as well as idiosyncratic and arbitrary in separating the sheep from the goats and the saved from the unsaved. This God was cruel, utterly inscrutable, and mysterious, beyond human fathoming.

Those who have not found the heaven below will fail of it above.

—EMILY DICKINSON

Meanwhile, Dickinson experienced Divinity in her marrow and saw herself as possessing the vocation of Poet, just as Jesus had been the Carpenter. But even with that awareness, the Almighty One hid the Divine face, coming to her only in nocturnal wrestling, never revealing God's true identity. Still, Dickenson wrestled throughout her life, finding God in the beauty of Nature and poetic inspiration.

Dickinson felt that God's arm was "amputated" and unable to reach humanity in its need. Dickinson believed in God, experienced the Holy, but never fully trusted the God of religious systems. All her life she remained a religious outsider, despite feeling God-filled as she looked at the Divine handiwork in the birth of each morning and the close of each day. Her faith—her encounters with God—were fraught with uncertainty and ceaseless change, vacillating between faith and doubt.

She had the loving agnosticism that was characteristic of the founding parents of the United States, healthy for a nation that legally levels the playing field among the various religious traditions. The affirmation of pluralism requires a sense of the many-sidedness of the Holy, as well as the finite perspectives of human beings. There must be room for doubters, skeptics, and atheists as well as faithful believers of all traditions if the United States is to fulfill its founding parents' vision.

Dickinson spent virtually all her adult life in the family homestead. After the death of her father, she never left its environs; some historians suggest she suffered from agoraphobia. She met the world through occasional visiters and the extensive and evocative letters she sent and received from intimate friends and family members. She never married but appeared to have had at least one intimate male companion; other Dickinson scholars believe she was in love with her sister-in-law.

Unable are the loved to die. For love is immortality.

—EMILY DICKINSON

Death often touched her life, as was the norm of the times, and yet, despite the universality of death, it was then, as now, always an affront to the human spirit. She understood we are infinite in spirit yet bound to the flesh. The best we can hope is to limp forward as Jacob did after wrestling with the inscrutable God.

Emily Dickinson died in 1886, at age fifty-five, most likely from acute hypertension and kidney disease. After her death, she might have sunk into obscurity, known only as an eccentric neighbor and relative, if not for her sister's unexpected discovery of her poems and consequent willingness to share Dickinson's spirit with the world. Her poetry is her proclamation and invitation to embrace the Holy with all our doubts and questions.

The Mysticism of Struggle

Emily Dickinson was both intimate with and ambivalent in her relationship with the Holy. She wrote often of wonder, awe, and amazement at the flora and fauna of Amherst and the grandeur of God in the heavens above and the surrounding countryside. She experienced God as the Great Mystery beyond all description, whose intimate energy gives life to all Creation.

Although Dickinson wrote plenty about God, she recognized the limits of both speech and experience. Our images of God are finite and so are our experiences. As the apostle Paul says, we look into a mirror dimly, and even at our best, we know only in part. Accordingly, we must both be humble and willing to revise our understandings of God in light of new experiences and intuitions.

> On subjects of which we know nothing, or should I say *Beings* . . . we both believe and dis-believe an hundred Times an Hour, which keeps Believing nimble.[34]

Yet, the Creative God is also, at least in the minds of many worshippers, the Destroyer, the One from whose hands mortality and sickness come. Without consent, we are brought into the world, condemned for sins we did not commit. At least that was the message of the revival preachers, who dangled salvation and damnation before their congregants, describing the undeserved love of God while proclaiming humanity as sinners in the hands of angry God. In describing this relationship with God, Dickinson wrote:

> *God is indeed a jealous God—*
> *He cannot bear to see*
> *That we would rather not with Him*
> *But with each other play.* (Poem 1719)

Dickinson was drawn to God. She experienced the amazing reality of the universe, the stars above, and the natural beauties of Amherst. At the same time, however, she was repulsed by the theologians and preachers she had heard in her younger days, men who described God as arbitrary, wrathful, and destructive. She felt at home with Jesus, who knew the meaning of suffering and grief, but the Almighty Potentate of Calvinist preaching offended her both spiritually and theologically. In a letter, Dickinson advised a friend to experience Holiness in her heart, not in church, "come with me this morning, in the church within our hearts, where . . . the Preacher whose name is Love— shall intercede for us."[35]

> *Some keep the Sabbath going to Church I keep it, staying at Home*
> *With a Bobolink for a Chorister*
> *And an Orchard, for a Dome.*
>
> —EMILY DICKINSON

Dickinson internalized the theological struggle between affirming God the Friend and fearing God the Enemy. While she believed Jesus is intimate with our struggles and is always ready to meet us with open arms, the Majestic God of the Calvinists (and today's conservative Christianity) both embraces and condemns, drawing some to Christ and leaving others, by Divine fiat, outside the precincts of salvation. In contrast, Dickinson believed, despite all her doubts, that God has made us both infinite and finite, a little lower than Divinity yet tethered to mortality. We can range the universe yet perish with dementia and unbearable pain.

Dickinson embodied Rudolf Otto's description of our encounters with the Holy as mysterious, awesome, and alluring. At the end of our journeys, we are left with a sense of the infinite distance between humanity and Divinity.

> *Their Height in Heaven comforts not–*
> *Their glory–nought to me–*
> *'Twas best imperfect–as it was–*
> *I'm finite–I can't see– . . .*
> *Better than larger values–*
> *That show however true–*
> *This timid life of evidence*
> *Keeps pleading–"I don't know." (Poem 696)*

My own theological journey parallels that of Dickinson's. I was raised in a small-town Baptist church, where youth and adults alike were regularly invited to accept Jesus as their personal savior. I "came forward"–accepted Jesus– at a revival meeting, led by the cowboy evangelist Leonard

Eilers. Then, just a few years later, I could no longer accept the faith of my childhood. The God of my youth was too small and vindictive, too arbitrary and exclusive, for my growing universalism and appreciation of other spiritual traditions. I left the church entirely, turning to Hinduism, Buddhism, Transcendentalism, and the immediacy of psychedelic experiences. My encounter as a college student with Paul Tillich's *Dynamics of Faith* enabled me once again to embrace the Christian faith. When Tillich asserted that authentic faith included and embraced experiences of doubt, I was able to come home to Jesus. I no longer needed to "know" or to affirm the "orthodoxy" of my youth to be faithful to God. The depth of faith, Tillich wrote, involves both struggles with unbelief and the certainty of belief.

> *In the name of the bee*
> *and of the butterfly*
> *and of the breeze, amen!*
>
> —EMILY DICKINSON

For Dickinson, this same quest for immediacy beyond doctrine was at the heart of her mysticism. The human spirit changes from moment to moment, drawing near and then turning from Divinity. As Jacob's wrestles and hangs on to God until he receives a blessing, he reflects the deepest piety that's not content with easy answers or superficial spirituality. He—like Emily Dickinson—embraces God in the struggle to believe. He holds on to God despite the pain of death, unanswered prayer, and finitude.

Awesome and awe-full, the world compelled Dickinson to believe, but more than that, to experience the currents of Divinity in her life. Her belief was of the same faithful agnosticism of the father, whose epileptic son was healed by Jesus when he said, "I believe, help my unbelief" (Mark 9:24). God is here, but the Divine is more than we can fathom or imagine. The universe declares the glory of God, and although the *kataphatic* way invites us to affirm God's presence in the bees, flowers, and meadows dear to Dickinson, this same wondrous immensity also compels us to be *apophatic* in our spirituality, recognizing that God will always be a Deep Mystery and Dazzling Darkness.[36]

This holy relativism is the salt of democracy and the quest for the "more perfect union." We are not there yet. Our visions are greater than our achievements. The human condition is always both ambiguous and mysterious, and while we must champion our beliefs, it is dangerous to democracy, as we have seen in the twenty-first century, to adhere to binary in-and-out, truth-and-error, and saved-and-unsaved visions that lead to the devaluation and persecution of anyone we perceive different from ourselves in belief, lifestyle, or politics.

Beauty and Ecstasy

If God is to be found anywhere, God encounters us in moments of awe, wonder, beauty, and ecstasy in which our finite "touches the universe" and we experience the holiness of life. Dickinson exclaimed,

> 'Tis Miracle before Me–then–
> 'Tis Miracle behind–between– (Poem 721)

"God is here" in the buzzing bee, the woodlands and hills, and the breaking of the day (Poem 155). "Paradise is no Journey because it is within."[37] The tragedy of life is to miss out on the bliss of Beauty in the midst of time. "Thin places" are everywhere for those with eyes to see. Dickinson finds "ecstasy in living—the mere sense of living is joy enough."[38]

Discovering the tragic beauty of life takes us beyond ourselves to identify with the universe, whole and parts, in its wonder, beauty, and cosmic indifference.

> *The Fact that Earth is Heaven—*
> *Whether Heaven is Heaven or not* (Poem 140)

As a child, Dickinson "met no one but angels" when she walked the woodlands near her home. She wrote: "Take everything away from me, but leave me ecstasy" (Poem 1640). In such an amazing world, ecstasy and wonder are our birthright and should be at the heart of the ministry of the church and the educational process. "Awe is the first hand that is held out to us. I always ran home with awe when a child, if anything befell me."[39] Dickinson worried about the loss of a mystic's or child's sense wonder.

> *Whoever disenchants*
> *A single Human soul*
> *By failure of irreverence*
> *Is guilty of the whole.* (Poem 1451)

The Finite Infinite

Ecstasy takes us beyond ourselves. We are no longer isolated selves, bereft of resources. The whole universe flows in and though us. We are finite, fallible, and mortal, yet we are also only a little lower than the angels. We are finite infinities, grounded in Divinity, and uniquely ourselves in relationship to Divinity. We are a drop in the ocean of holiness, whose momentary lifetime is unique, centered, and possessing an integrity that even God cannot destroy.

Dickinson rebelled against Calvinistic concepts of moral depravity and predestination to salvation or damnation. She believed Divine energy gives life, and our lives are characterized by agency and interdependence. Grounded in the awesome power of the universe, children of stardust and children of the Big Bang, our soul is "Finite infinity" (Poem 1695). Yes, our lives are "small," Dickinson wrote, but they participate in Infinity and Eternity:

> Swelled—like Horizons—in my vest
> And I sneered—softly—"small." (Poem 124)

Still, Dickinson struggled to affirm the self-transcendence that makes a claim against God. Like Jacob, she wrestled with God and survived. Like Jacob, she was wounded and blessed.

The meager drop, hardly worth notice in relationship to galaxies beyond number, still possesses a center worthy of affirmation and amazement:

The Drop that wrestles in the Sea—
Forgets her own locality—
As I toward Thee—
She knows herself an incense small—
Yet small—she sighs—if All is All—
How larger be?
The Ocean smiles at her Conceit –
But she forgetting Amphitrite—
Pleads—"Me"? (Poem 284)

Even in the immensity of the universe—and the wildness of the sea—Amphitrite (the goddess of the sea) and the God of the Universe must take account of each soul. "Soul selects her own Society" (Poem 303). Even though Dickinson didn't pray in traditional ways, her own spiritual stature enabled her to sing, in the spirit of Whitman, the song of herself.[40]

In recognizing the soul's infinity, Dickinson affirmed the significance of the most ordinary acts. Our care for others expands our own sense of wonder and awakens others to the awesomeness of themselves and all Creation.

If I can stop one heart from breaking
I shall not live in vain
If I can ease one Life the Aching
Or cool one Pain
Or help one fainting Robin
Unto his Nest again,
I shall not live in Vain. (Poem 919)

Prayerful Questioning

A few years back, I had an encounter that changed the shape of my spiritual life. I was taking a pre-dawn walk in Springfield, Massachusetts, a book under my arm. As I approached a bus stop, a man there, thinking I had a Bible, called out "Jeremiah 33:3!" I was actually carrying *The Complete Poems of Emily Dickinson*, but later, I looked up the passage from the Bible: "Call to me and I will answer you, and will tell you great and hidden things that you have not known." I took his comments as revelatory, and since then, I have made a practice of calling upon God with my questions and uncertainties.

Emily Dickinson would have reveled in such a synchronous encounter. Although she left the church, primarily due to doctrinal issues and, I believe, its privilege of certain forms of spirituality as indicative of authentic faith, Dickinson was a person of faith in the spirit of both Jacob and the twentieth-century theologian Paul Tillich. She saw holiness everywhere. The beauty of the universe and the spirit of radical amazement were at the heart of her experience. She could not easily accept orthodox explanations of the universe, human life, mortality, and sin—but she experienced God in her poems and revelation in the world around her. The Holy was also found in her quest for answers. She cried out to God, and while she did not receive clear-cut answers, her prayers turned to songs and poems.

> *Faith—is the pierless bridge supporting what We see unto the scene that we do not.*
>
> —EMILY DICKINSON

Now, see if you can do the same. In the spirit of Jeremiah 33:3, cry out to God. Let your concerns become prayers. Let your doubts lead to queries. Seek prayerfully and you will find—whether you seek guidance for your personal life or your role as a citizen—and you will often be surprised by the discovery. God is as present in the struggle as in the calm, as alive in the pain as in the comfort. Take time to share your doubts with both God and trusted spiritual companions. Let your questions and struggles become avenues of grace and revelation.

Prayer of Awareness and Transformation

Holy One, help me to cry out for answers.
Help me to plead for change.
The world is awesome, yet awe-full;
it is breathtaking in beauty,
and yet we are frightened and overwhelmed
by sights of forest fires, collapsing glaciers,
and starving children in war-torn lands.
"Why?" we ask. "Is there no end to human deathfulness?"
Help us to take both our pain and joy
to you in prayer, O Listening God,
and give us enough light for the next step,
enough inspiration to challenge the evils of our time.
In the name of the "tender pioneer," we pray.

6

JOHN WOOLMAN

The Mysticism of the Moral Arc

To consider humanity other than kinfolk . . .
plainly supposes a darkness of understanding.

—JOHN WOOLMAN

frican American mystic, theologian, and social activist Howard Thurman (whose mystic vision we'll address in chapter 10) asserts that "social action, therefore, is an expression of resistance against whatever tends to, or separates one, from the experience of God, who is the ground of [our] being."[41] In other words, the mystic's encounter with the Living God, who infuses all Creation with life, energy, and beauty, inspires the quest to establish a social order in which everyone has opportunities to experience God's fullness in their lives. Recognizing the interdependence of life and the social nature of spiritual experience, mystics challenge every social, political, and economic structure that demeans humankind, preventing them from experiencing the Divine glory of being fully alive.

John Woolman (1720–1772) exemplified the unity of spiritual experience and social action. As a Quaker, he believed God's light was the deepest reality of every human being. No human—regardless of race, nation of origin, gender and sexuality, or previous behavior—was devoid of "the true light, which enlightens everyone" (John 1:9). Belief and experience lead to actions that promote the well-being of all God's children.

Woolman's recognition of God's universal presence led him to become a leader in the Abolitionist movement, affirm just relationships with Indigenous people, and champion humane treatment of nonhuman animals. Historian David Sox notes, "If I were asked to date the birth of racial consciousness in its present form, I think I should put it on the twenty-sixth day of the eighth month of the year 1758—the day John Woolman in a public meeting denounced Negro slavery."[42] Woolman's shaping of Quaker

There is a principle which is pure, placed in the human mind, which in different places and ages hath had different names. It is, however, pure and proceeds from God. It is deep and inward, confined to no forms of religion nor excluded from any, where the heart stands in perfect sincerity. In whomsoever this takes root and grows, of what nation soever, they become family in the best sense of the expression.

—JOHN WOOLMAN

attitudes toward slavery catalyzed the Abolitionist movement in the United States.

Woolman's Life

Born in New Jersey in 1720, the fourth of six children, Woolman was raised in a devout Quaker family. He embraced the
Quaker vision of reality as his own spiritual pathway. He
was, he wrote:

> Early convinced in my mind that true religion con-
> sisted in an inward life, wherein the heart doth love
> and reverence God the Creator and learn to exercise
> true justice and goodness, not only toward all men
> but also toward the brute creatures; that the mind
> was moved on an inward principle to love God as
> an invisible, incomprehensible being, on the same
> principle it was moved to love him in all his manifes-
> tations in the visible world; that as by his breath the
> flame of life was kindled in all animal and sensible
> creatures to say we love God as unseen and at the
> same time exercise cruelty toward the least creature
> moving by his life, or the life derived from him, was
> a contradiction in itself.

Gifted with a sensitive conscience, Woolman later
recalled a pivotal experience from his childhood. As a child,
he had thrown stones at a mother robin, killing her. Realizing her chicks would not survive without their mother, he
proceeded to kill them as well. Later that day, however, his

cruelty weighed on him. Years later, as he wrote of his childhood in his *Journal*, he said: "I mention this . . . , to show How God the parent of All Creatures hath placed that in the human mind which doth Instruct and incite to exercise Goodness towards all his creatures."[43]

From childhood, Woolman was "haunted" by God (to use Flannery O'Conner's imagery) through what he described as Divine openings, interpreted as messages from God, in the form of dreams, insights, and inspirations. These spiritual experiences, as well as the pangs of conscience beginning in childhood, eventually shaped his spiritual activism and commitment to stand with the oppressed, impoverished, and powerless.

> *To turn all the treasures we possess into the channel of universal love becomes the business of our lives.*
>
> —JOHN WOOLMAN

Nineteenth-century Unitarian minister Theodore Parker asserted that "the arc of the moral universe is long, but it bends toward justice." This is surely true in the evolving morality of communities and nations, and it is also true of our own lives, if we allow our conscience to open to God's vision of Shalom for all Creation.

When he was a young man, Woolman entered business as a shopkeeper, bookkeeper, and legal transcriber, where he quickly gained his employer's trust. His employer asked him to sell an enslaved woman, however, and Woolman's conscience objected. Writing legal documents was part of his job, but he felt uneasy at participating in "writing an instrument of slavery for one of my fellow creatures." Woolman knew he needed to inform his employer that enslavement was a practice "inconsistent with the Christian religion." He wrote out the bill of sale, while sharing his moral uneasiness with his employer, but he regretted doing so.

From then on, Woolman would no longer participate directly in the slave trade, and he sought to convince anyone who came to him for professional services to free the people they had enslaved. Eventually, Woolman convinced Quakers to abandon slavery in all its forms, whether trade or ownership. He inspired a serious ongoing debate about abolition in the United States.

Once Woolman recognized his complicity in the evils of slavery, he sought to extricate himself as much as possible from the oppression he deplored. He recognized, as Thomas Merton did two centuries later, that there are no innocent bystanders. If he were alive today, Woolman would affirm the insights of Critical Race Theory, which sees racial injustice as structural and systemic. He would no doubt see slavery and the genocide of Indigenous peoples as the United States' "original sin"—and he would seek through personal and political means to repair the damage done through centuries of racial and economic injustice.

May we look upon our treasure, the furniture of our houses, and our garments, and try to discover whether the seeds of war have nourishment in these our possessions.

–JOHN WOOLMAN

Over time, as Woolman came to recognize the relationship between the use of dye and the slave trade, he changed his attire to simple, undyed garments. Later, he quit selling any products connected with slavery, such as rum and molasses, and eventually, he stopped even using them. He had realized that our lifestyles are implicitly or explicitly connected with the suffering of others. Even our quest for justice and a simpler lifestyle may have unintended effects on our neighbors' economic well-being.

Woolman's recognition that the light of God shines in the enslaved person as well as the enslaver led him to become a leader in the emerging Abolitionist movement. He focused primarily on his Quaker brothers' and sisters' complicity in slavery, whether through enslavement, trade, or lifestyle choices, and he walked thousands of miles in the South and New England to challenge slaveholding and slave trading. He chose to travel by foot as an affirmation of his solidarity with people in economic distress; the presence of God's light in all people compelled him to place himself in the same position as "the least of these" among his sisters and brothers. He later sailed to England, where he walked the countryside and spoke passionately to Quaker gatherings, urging England to abandon the slave trade.

Over the next several years, Woolman expanded his ethical circle to include Indigenous communities. He saw America's First Nations as beloved children of God, not savages, and he believed he could learn from the simplicity of their way of life and their affirmative approach to the nonhuman world. He recognized that God's love embraced enslaved and Indigenous people as much as the white person, and that each individual deserved respect and affirmation personally and politically.

Woolman's quest to follow the path of Jesus led him to civil disobedience by refusing to pay the war tax that funded British involvement in the French and Indian War (1754-

1763). Nevertheless, when he was asked to board a group of British soldiers, he supplied them with food and lodging at no cost to the government. He believed hospitality without gain, even to soldiers whose actions he opposed, was a way to recognize God's presence in everyone.

Be careful that the love of gain draw us not into any business which may weaken our love of our Heavenly Father or bring unnecessary trouble to any of His creatures.

–JOHN WOOLMAN

Woolman's final sojourn took him to England, where he was initially an object of ridicule among upper-class British Quakers due to his simple, homespun outfit. As his fellow Quakers heard his insightful and passionate case for Abolition, however, they found a kindred spirit who awakened them to the inner light in themselves and in people they had initially judged as their inferiors.

On his way to England, he had chosen to travel in steerage with the crew rather than the stateroom that had been arranged for him. His commitment to overcoming class distinctions during his trans-Atlantic voyage most likely physically weakened him, compromising his immune system. He died from smallpox at age fifty-one in 1782.

Inner Light, Outer Behavior

At the heart of Quaker spirituality is the affirmation that God's light shines in and through every person. There is something of God—an inner light, the light that "enlightens all" (John 1:9)—in each of us, regardless of race, age, nation of origin, gender identity, or any other quality. John Woolman believed God's Presence in every life requires us to treat each person with respect. Every human being is the subject of God's love.

In reflecting on slavery, Woolman asserted: "These are the people who have made no agreement to serve us. . . . These are the souls for whom Christ has died. For our conduct toward them, we must answer to God who shows no partiality."

Woolman's recognition of God's presence in enslavers as well as those they enslaved inspired him to challenge slavery, speaking the truth in love to those who participated in it. He believed that a peaceful rather than combative approach to conflict awakened the inner light of those whose practices he challenged. Like Martin Luther King Jr. two centuries later, Woolman believed injustice harms the oppressor as well as the victim and that appealing to the "better angels" of the oppressor's nature can lead to ethical and social transformation.

In a time of religious polarization, Woolman perceived something of God in the experiences and practices of the various forms of Christianity:

The Holy Spirit doth open and direct our minds and as we faithfully yield to it, our prayers unite with the will of our Heavenly Father.

–JOHN WOOLMAN

From an inner purifying springs a lively operative desire for the good of others . . . The outward modes of worship are various, but wheresover people are true worshippers of Jesus Christ, it is from the operation of his spirit upon their hearts, first purifying them and then giving them a feeling sense of the condition of others.

God's light is actively at work in our lives and the world, regardless of our station in life, economic and social status, race, or denomination. While God speaks directly to each person, we can more fully hear God's voice when we take time for silent listening. As Woolman wrote:

> The necessity of an inward stillness hath before these exercises appeared clear to my mind. In true silence, strength is renewed, the mind herein is weaned from all things but as they may be joined in the Divine Will; and a lowliness of outward living opposite of worldly honor, becomes truly acceptable to us . . . in the weaning of the mind from all things but as they may be enjoyed in the Divine Will, the pure light shines into the soul.

During a time of illness, Woolman had a vision—perhaps a near-death experience—in which his small self "died" in intimate relationship with God and all Creation. In the darkness of illness, Woolman's inner light joined with God's universal light, embodied in all Creation.

> I saw a mass of matter of a dull, gloomy color between the south and the east. I was informed that this mass was human beings in as great misery as they could be and live. I was mixed with them and henceforth might

not consider myself as a distinct or separate being. I remained in this state for several hours. I heard a soft, melodious voice, more pure and harmonious than any I had heard with my ears before. I believed it was the voice of an angel who spoke to the other angels. The words were "John Woolman is dead." . . . I was then carried in spirit to the mines where poor oppressed people were digging treasures for those called Christians and heard them blaspheme the name of Christ. . . .

Then, as he lay in stillness, Woolman felt God's power within him preparing him to speak of his new identity: "I have been crucified with Christ; and it is no longer I who live, but it is Christ who lives in me." In dying to his own will, John Woolman became identified with God's will and God's presence in all Creation.

Opening to the inner light, we grow with Jesus in "wisdom and stature" (Luke 2:52). We move from individual self-interest to care for all Creation. As our spirits expand, other people's interests become as important as our own. We become one with all life, experiencing the joys and sorrows of others as our own joys and sorrows, and seeking the well-being of all Creation as necessary to our own wholeness and well-being.

Reverence for Life

Because of John Woolman's affirmation of the Divine Presence in the nonhuman as well as the human world, he has been described as the Saint Francis of Assisi of North

America. He believed God's love and presence are broadcast throughout all Creation. The suffering of nonhuman animals touches the heart of God and should inspire our respect for our fellow creatures. Woolman wrote: "Thus the one whose tender mercies are over all his works has placed a principle in the human mind that incites us to practice goodness toward every living creature."

Moreover, Woolman said, God's "breath the flame of life was kindled in all animal and sensible creatures." To say we love God and at the same time exercise cruelty toward the least creature whose life is derived from God is a contradiction in itself. Because God "cares and provides for all his Creatures . . . we feel a desire to lessen the distresses of the afflicted and increase the happiness of the Creation." Honoring God leads to honoring the Earth. God's beloved Creation belongs to God and not us, and we must be stewards rather than destroyers of our planet.

Woolman advocated a type of sustainable agriculture, based on simplicity and care for the soil. He taught that care for the commons—the Earth itself—rather than the quest for wealth should guide agricultural practices. "The produce of the earth," Woolman believed, "is a gift from our gracious Creator to the inhabitants, and to impoverish the earth now to support outward greatness appears to be an injury to the succeeding age." The light within and the light beyond are one light. Love of ourselves, others, and Nature reflects God's presence in all people and Creation, calling us, even in our fallibility, to reverence for the Earth and all its creatures.

Spiritual Decluttering

Decluttering has become a fad in recent years. Many people have discovered that rather than possessing their possessions, their possessions have come to possess them. Our wants have become needs, and this has made our lives more complicated and our finances more challenging. We are victims of what the Quakers describe as "cumber," possessions and activities that clutter our daily schedules and household chores.

Cumber can also apply to the complexities of daily life. Parents and grandparents spend hours on the road, taking their children to sports practices, music lessons, and extracurricular activities. There is little time for a day of Sabbath rest in a summer filled with ten weeks of camps and sports practices. As Winnie the Pooh's companion Christopher Robin laments, growing up means the loss of afternoons simply "doing nothing."

Thus He whose tender mercies are over all His works . . . incites to exercise goodness towards every living creature; and this being singly attended to, people become tenderhearted and sympathizing; but when frequently and totally rejected, the mind becomes shut up in a contrary disposition.

—JOHN WOOLMAN

Our daily projects, children's activities, and household conveniences are not in themselves evil, but they can be the sources of unnecessary stress on ourselves and our relationships. They can also be factors in environmental destruction, especially through extravagant consumption and the use of fossil fuels. We need to look mindfully at our lives to ascertain what truly gives us joy, what we need to live happily—and what is unnecessary, time-consuming, and ecologically unsound.

As I began my "retirement," I sought to simplify my life in terms of schedule and largesse. I thinned down my book collection, as I already mentioned; I also pruned my closet of clothing I no longer wear; and I simplified my daily schedule to focus on what is truly important—friendship, mission, justice-seeking, creativity, spirituality, and family.

In a similar way, spiritual decluttering was at the heart of John Woolman's spirituality. Although he was a smart and successful businessperson, the burden of too many responsibilities weighed him down. He realized that:

> *Do we feel an affectionate Regard to Posterity; and are we employed to promote their Happiness? Do our Minds, in Things outward, look beyond our own Dissolution; and are we contriving for the Prosperity of our Children after us? Let us then, like wise Builders, lay the Foundation deep.*
>
> —JOHN WOOLMAN

> A humble man with the blessing of the Lord might live on a little, and where the heart was set on greatness, success in business did not satisfy the craving, but in common with an increase in wealth the desire of wealth increased.

Further, Woolman sought to simplify his business responsibilities because mercantile success often led to hurry and ethical compromise. The excuse "it's just business" has led to business practices that place profit over people, layoffs that devastate families and communities, and millions of working people living in poverty despite long hours of employment. Emphasis on profit-making often fails to consider the ecological and personal costs of business practices. Recognizing the pitfalls of the profit motive, Woolman asserted:

> In the love of money and in the wisdom of the world, business is proposed, then in the urgency of affairs, pushed forward, and the mind in this state cannot discern the good and perfect will of God concerning us . . . the mind remains entangled and the shining light of life into the soul is obstructed.

Because of the interdependence of all life, it is impossible to be an innocent bystander—but we can, like Woolman, live our lives according to our deepest values, guided by our vision of God's Peaceable Realm. We can begin to live simply so that others can simply live, as we evaluate how our daily lives match up with what is truly important to us.

In the spirit of the Examen (the spiritual tool created by Ignatius of Loyola that gives daily opportunities to examine our consciences), ask yourself the following questions:

- What are your deepest spiritual and interpersonal values?

- What brings you the greatest joy?

- What does personal fulfillment mean to you?

- What is the impact of your lifestyle on other people and on the planet?

- What daily practices complicate your life and lead to unnecessary stress?

- How can you pare down your possessions, responsibilities, and schedules to live more abundantly in terms of relationships, spiritual values, and joy?

- What steps do you need to take to live a more environmentally healthy life?

There are many possible responses to these questions, based on our ages, work situations, size of our families, places of residence, health conditions, and so forth. Still, regardless of individual circumstances, we can find greater joy by using these questions to "center down" on what is important, while we disengage from practices that harm our health, relationships, spiritual lives, and environment. We can let go of possessions and socially acceptable busyness to experience greater peace of mind, contentment with our lifestyle, and solidarity with the Earth.

Prayer of Awareness and Transformation

God of all Creation,
awaken me to the beauty of this world.
Guide me in the ordering of my life.
Help me discern the difference between wants and needs
so that I might live mindfully,
contributing to the well-being of my family,
community, planet, and myself.
Let me live joyfully and simply so that others
might share the blessings of abundant life
in body, mind, and spirit.

7

ANN LEE
AND THE SHAKERS

In Search of the Divine Feminine

God is a dual person, male and female.

−SHAKER DOCTRINE

God is always more than we can ever imagine. Though traces of Divinity are found in every creature and any moment can be an open door to the Infinite, the God of the Universe can never be encompassed by human symbols, words, scriptures, or rituals. Still, our language and culture are the lenses through which we reflect and embody the Infinite in finite space and time. Human experiences and cultural values always shape God's call to a greater or lesser degree by. Our cultures and faith traditions are the source of both limitation and possibility. Tradition provides order and the springboard for encountering God; it may also imprison us in cramped and partial experiences and descriptions of the Holy.

Given the interplay of infinite and finite in time and space, America has room for a variety of spiritual experiences. Spirituality is always forward-looking, honoring the past even as it looks toward far horizons with the affirmation, "There is more."

In the Western world, masculine images of God have dominated theological reflection, often to the exclusion of the feminine dimensions of Divinity and experience. The belief in a male God has undergirded male clerical domination, subordinating the feminine aspects of religious experience and denying spiritual leadership to women—despite the fact that women have been spiritual leaders, mystics, and cultural creatives throughout history. The spiritual leadership of women has often been neglected and marginalized in the unfolding of American religious traditions. This has also been true of women's roles in politics, property, and economics.

While many people have rightly recognized the patriarchal nature of the biblical tradition that's reflected in the Jewish, Christian, and Muslim religious traditions, the Hebraic tradition from which the Abrahamic faiths emerged also affirmed a God beyond gender and yet inclusive of both feminine and masculine dimensions.

The first Genesis creation story speaks of an emerging universe, guided by Divine Wisdom. The image of God in humankind reflects a Divinity whose nature embraces both male and female:

Then God said, "Let us make humankind in our image, according to our likeness; and let them have dominion over the fish of the sea, and over the birds of the air, and over the cattle, and over all the wild animals of the earth, and over every creeping thing that creeps upon the earth." So God created humankind in his image, in the image of God he created them; male and female he created them. (Genesis 1:26-27)

The Divine Unity is both male and female, interdependent and equal, and present as the foundation of human life. While the second creation story (Genesis 2:4-24) appears to subordinate the woman to her male counterpart, the perceptive reader sees that the feminine and masculine require each other to be fulfilled; Adam proclaims that the woman is "bone of my bone and flesh of my flesh" (Genesis 2:23). This affirmation reveals the intimate and essential relatedness of male and female. The woman's male companion cannot flourish without her! Nor can she flourish without him! In today's world of gender fluidity, we see reflected God's wondrous unity-in-diversity. The amazing expanse of human experience and sexuality goes far beyond the binary.

The Shakers, known formally as the United Society of Believers in Christ's Second Coming, believed the Divine encompassed both male and female, and that salvation required the recognition of both aspects of Divinity. Unlike people who proclaim that maleness defines Divinity, and only males can be channels of God's wisdom, the Shakers saw Ann Lee as the feminine manifestation of Divine

Wisdom, inaugurating the fulfillment of Christ's promise to humankind.

An illiterate woman from a working-class background, Ann Lee is, at first glance, an unlikely manifestation of God's revelation to humankind. However, her spiritual experience called her to be a Divine messenger—a "spirit person," to use the language of Marcus Borg. This unlikely channel of revelation reflects the life of another "spirit person," Jesus of Nazareth, born in stable, celebrated by humble shepherds, the child of working-class parents, in an oppressed nation.

> *By crying to God continually I traveled out of my loss.*
>
> —ANN LEE

The Life of Ann Lee

Born on February 29, 1736, Ann Lee grew up in working-class Manchester, England, the second of a blacksmith-mechanic's eight children. Ann went to work at an early age, most likely cutting velvet and making fur hats in the growing clothing-trade industry; then, as a teenager, she assumed maternal responsibilities for her younger siblings when her mother died. A few years later, Lee took a job as a cook at a local hospital for people suffering from mental illness. Ann Lee never learned to read and the only extant document from her hand is the "X" she signed on her marriage certificate. In her twenties, Lee married and gave birth to four children in succession, all of whom died in childhood.

In 1758, Ann Lee encountered John and Jane Wardley, luminaries in the emerging British Shaker movement. These

Shaking Quakers shared the Quaker affirmation that God is present in every human heart and can be experienced directly, without priestly mediation. They went beyond the typical Quaker experience in their ecstatic worship, singing, shouting, and shaking at the instigation of God's Spirit. At the heart of the Wardleys' movement was the act of confession in which people confessed their sins to the community as a prelude to achieving Christian perfection.

Ann Lee's relationship with the English Shakers transformed her. After several years of soul searching, she realized God had addressed her personally, calling her to be "Ann the Word," God's feminine representative and witness, along with the male Jesus, to prophesy to a world hell-bent on destruction.

Her fellow Shakers and people in the wider community began to recognize her unique relationship with God. Thankful Barce, one of Lee's contemporaries, asserted, "If I ever saw the image of Christ displayed in human clay, I saw it in Mother Ann."[44] Her followers believed that "Christ did verily make his second appearance in Ann Lee"; a Shaker leader described her relationship with God with the following affirmation:

> We recognize the Christ spirit, the expression of Deity, first manifested in its fullness in Jesus of Nazareth. We also regard Ann Lee as the first to receive in this latter day this internal realization that this same Divine Spirit which was in Jesus might dwell, within the consciousness of any man, woman, or child.[45]

As I noted earlier, Ann Lee was a spirit person, a human being who directly experienced the Divine. She was able to convey the experience of Divine immediacy to others, thus giving birth to a new American spiritual movement.

In the 1760s, Lee took over the spiritual leadership of the Shakers, who continued worshipping in the Spirit with dance, singing, and ecstatic tongues. After a vision, Ann Lee made celibacy central to Shaker experience. She believed the lusts of the flesh—sexuality, greed, avarice—bind us to the Earth and interfere with the experience of God's fullness in human life. Worldly success, property, marriage, family, and sexuality not only separate us from God, she said; they also create social inequalities and damage the human community. Even the most generous of marriages creates an informal in-group, in which certain people receive preferential treatment over others. In reflecting on Shaker celibacy, Lee asserted:

You can never enter the kingdom of God with hardness against any one, for God is love, and if you love God you will love one another.

—ANN LEE

> Sin is the glorification of self! Only through celibacy can true Godliness be achieved. You must forsake the marriage of the flesh, or you can't be married to the Lamb.[46]

Her commitment to celibacy as a pathway to God eventually led to the dissolution of her marriage. Shaker "communism," grounded in their interpretations of the early church's commandment to hold all things in common, necessitated an egalitarian society in which privilege and preference did not interfere with the common good.

Shaker ecstasy and lifestyle led to persecution in both England and America. Their worship style, denial of marriage, and celibacy were viewed as threats to both church and state. Lee, along with other Shaker leaders, were imprisoned for their beliefs. They were accused of desecrating the Sabbath with their lively worship, and Lee's affirmation of her spiritual companionship with Jesus was seen as blasphemy. Her unwavering commitment to sharing God's presence with others was met with violence even in her own household: her brother beat her because of her beliefs.

In 1774, Ann Lee—like Paul and Peter in the Book of Acts—experienced a vision with the accompanying command to spread the gospel to a foreign land, America. She and eight followers boarded a dilapidated ship, the *Mariah*, bound for New York. On the voyage, the ship was caught in a storm. When the ship took on water, the captain was on the verge of giving up hope for their survival, but Lee consoled him with these words:

> Captain, be of good cheer, there shall not be a hair of our heads perish; we shall arrive safe in America. I was just now sitting by the mast, and I saw a bright angel of God, through whom I received this promise.[47]

Lee and her companions arrived in New York just as revolutionary fervor was escalating. Anything British was considered suspect, and for the next several years, the Shakers in America experienced poverty and persecution. Ann Lee was jailed, in part because of her British citizenship and the pacifism she and her companions espoused. She was considered both a spy and a witch, the latter term one that historically has often been applied to strong spirit-centered women.

The Shakers relocated to upstate New York, where they founded their first of many self-contained farms, "Niskeyuna." Recognizing the holiness of their Indigenous neighbors, they received guidance in agriculture and hunting from members of a nearby Mohawk community.

Lee's closeness to God inspired the lively worship among her followers. While preserving the Spirit-centered nature of worship, men and women danced in separate rows, experiencing God's energy moving through their cells and souls. As one simple hymn proclaims,

> *We love to dance, we love to sing,*
> *We love to taste the living spring,*
> *We love to feel our union flow,*
> *While round, and round, and round, we go.*[48]

Lee's spiritual egalitarianism was radical for her time. The Eternal Two, the male and female wholeness of God, she believed, is to be reflected in equal relationships between men and women. Moreover, celibacy liberated women from the burdens of childbearing and filial inferiority. In abandoning the sexual mores of her time, Lee asserted, "We are not called to be one thing or another—male or female, or young or old. We are called to show forth the Divine—to be all things to all people."[49]

Ann Lee died in 1784, having inspired and shaped communities throughout New England. By the mid-nineteenth century, the Shakers boasted six thousand members, but over the years, the movement, due to its celibate lifestyle, has dwindled to only one remaining active Shaker community. As of March 2024, two living Shakers remained at Sabbath Day Lake in New Gloucester, Maine.

The Vocation of Spirit Person

We have no direct writings from Ann Lee. Written accounts of her life, not unlike the Gospels, were not penned until thirty years after her death. Still, the portrait of Ann Lee from her followers reveals someone who embodied, if not Divinity in its fullness as traditional Shaker theology asserted, at least the characteristics of a spirit person, someone who directly experienced the holy and was able to convey that same experience to those around her.

Throughout her life, Ann Lee had visionary encounters with God. As a result of these encounters, she believed her words reflected God's word and wisdom for humankind. She was not unique, she asserted; she was simply like Jesus Christ, a reflection in human flesh of God's message for her time. Like her male counterpart, she said,

You have all had the privilege of being taught the way of God; and now you may all go home and be faithful with your hands.

—ANN LEE

her gifts of vision and wisdom were intended to upbuild the community as the Body of Christ, vivified by Christ's blood flowing through every member. As her followers opened themselves to her experience, they too became spirit people.

God is present everywhere, but God can choose to be present in extraordinary ways, inspiring and empowering unique revelations. The Shakers believed that the ever-present God "chose" Ann Lee to reveal God's feminine reality and establish God's Realm on Earth. God dwelt in her, the Shakers believed; her body was truly the temple, the shrine, of the Holy Spirit.

We don't have to share the belief that this was literally the case, nor accept that Lee was Christ's feminine counter-part, but we can still learn from her spiritual insights. She described her intimacy with Christ in terms of his presence in her as companion and spouse.

> It is not I that speaks; but Christ who dwells in me. . . . I have been in fine vallies [sic] with Christ as my lover. I am married to the Lord Jesus Christ. He is my head and my husband and I have no other! I have walked, hand in hand, with him in heaven.[50]

Lee was energized and activated by the indwelling Christ and could share this experience with others.

According to Ann Lee and her Shaker companions, God is both Father and Mother. Divinity moved through her to express the Motherhood of God. Because Christ must appear in every female, she taught, Christ must be revealed in a woman as well as in Jesus. Accordingly, she was "a chosen vessel, appointed by Divine Wisdom"[51] Like Jesus, she said, she was endowed with the power to transform cells as well as souls. One of her followers, Thankful Barce, reported that when their hands would brush against each other, "I instantly felt the power of God run through my whole body."[52]

Ann Lee's followers believed she channeled the same saving energy and wisdom that was present in Jesus. Her revelation fulfilled the wholeness of God's presence in humanity. A Shaker hymn proclaimed:

> The Father's high eternal throne
> Was never filled by one alone:
> There Wisdom holds the Mother's seat
> And is the Father's helper-meet.
> he vast creation was not made
> Without the fruitful Mother's Aid.

Prayerful Work

Although the origins of her message were heavenly, Ann Lee was intensely practical. The Word is made flesh in man and woman, Jesus and Ann, and in the Shaker community's daily life. Humans are God's witnesses in the world, she taught, through the purity of their lives and the quality of their work. She counseled her followers to "put your hands to work and hearts to God."[53]

Though viewed as otherworldly because of their religious practices and celibacy, Shakers believed their calling was to embody God's Realm, the Second Coming of Christ, on Earth. A good life, they said, involved recognizing that "labor is worship and prayer."[54] Thirty years ago, one of the few remaining Sabbath Day Lake Shakers noted, "Sweeping, like any other act you can do in the community, can have sacred proportions. Remember that all work is worship."[55] In that spirit, Ann Lee asserted that order in individual lives and in community is "the creator of beauty and the protection of our souls."[56]

Mystics don't wait to experience heaven at the hour of death. Instead, they know that each action and every task can reveal God's Realm on Earth. As citizens of God's Realm, Shakers sought to do everything for the glory of God. Because we live in God's constant presence, they believed we can be both heavenly minded and earthly good! The mystical Shakers sought to embody God's heaven in the holy here-and-now. Making a chair, sweeping a floor, or building a barn contributed to God's reign, in this world as well as the next.

Do all your work as though you had a thousand years to live; and as you would if you knew you must die tomorrow.

—ANN LEE[57]

In reflecting on the Shakers' integration of work and prayer, Trappist spiritual guide Thomas Merton wrote, "The peculiar grace of a Shaker chair is due to the fact that it was made by someone capable of believing that an angel might come and sit on it."[58] We are always in the presence of God, the Shakers taught, revealing Divinity to a greater or lesser extent by our faithfulness to the tasks placed before us.

Industrious, thrifty, and canny in business, Shakers were responsible for many inventions and innovations, including clothespins, circular saws, flat brooms, a wood-burning stove, an apple-parer, round barns, and a wheel-driven washing machine. Followers of God don't just live in the past of scripture or in a future in heaven; instead, they join God in creating a heavenly world of justice, equality, and joy in the here and now. Shaker simplicity meant willing but one thing in work, dance, prayer, and business: to actively live God's Realm, joining time and eternity in the present moment.

In the words of Shaker Elder Joseph Brackett:

'Tis the gift to be simple, 'tis the gift to be free
'Tis the gift to come down where we ought to be,
And when we find ourselves in the place just right,
'Twill be in the valley of love and delight.
When true simplicity is gained,
To bow and to bend we shan't be ashamed,
To turn, turn will be our delight,
Till by turning, turning we come 'round right.

The Foundation of Feminism

Ann Lee was one of the first people to speak out for the political and legal rights of women, and after her death, her followers built on her legacy. In the nineteenth century, Shaker Eldress Antoinette Doolittle wrote:

The momentous burden and weighty responsibility
of governing the country rests upon the shoulders,

and is entrusted to heads and hands of male rulers. The voice of woman is not heard in legislative halls—only as a special favor upon certain occasions, and by special request. Why this bondage and servitude on the part of woman? Has she no heart to feel? Is she destitute of reasoning powers, and unable to plead her own cause and the cause of her down trodden and oppressed sisters, who do them at the tribunals, where male rulers alone preside, judge and decide? Woman possesses latent powers that need to be brought into action, both for her own benefit and the good of humanity.[59]

In the twentieth century, Shakers continued to speak out for gender equality. Eldress Minnie Allen, for example, set aside the traditional Shaker values of isolation and a quiet internal life to advocate widely and publicly for women's rights and the humane treatment of animals. Regarding women's right to carry out political roles, she wrote:

First, who planned the Constitution and its laws? Men. Who have been its executors from first to last, in Senate and in House? Men. They have framed all our laws, have mended and amended them as they have thought proper, and what wonder? For ages back they had exercised sole authority in all offices of Church, quite unmindful of the fact that God had said "Let us create man in our own image." "Male and female created He them;" and also that every atom of the universe, from mineral ore to burning star includes, and is controlled by, dual forces.[60]

Prayerful Work

The Shakers believed in the ubiquitous presence of the All-Encompassing, Female and Male God. The distinction between sacred and secular is an illusion, they said. All people and events reflect the sacred and can be consecrated—made holy—in acts of worship.

God addresses us both in community and as unique individuals. As spiritual children of the Quakers, these "Shaking Quakers" affirmed the presence of God's inner light in all humankind. This led them to adopt and nurture orphans, awakening the children's spirits and providing them with a foundation for a holy life. The Shakers' beliefs also led them to purchase enslaved people in order to liberate them from the moral outrage of slavery.

Like the Celtic spiritual guides centuries before them, Shakers experienced "thin places" everywhere. They invite us to experience the holiness of everyday domestic tasks. Labor is worship and prayer; we can do every task to glorify God our Creator. From this perspective, the Shakers avoided the Marxist critique of capitalist economics, evidenced in the alienation of workers from the products they made, or products created solely for profit and without enduring value. In the spirit of Buddhism, the Shakers believed in

Do all the good you can,
in all the ways you can,
as often as you can,
to all the people you can.

—ANN LEE[61]

the principle of "right livelihood." They devoted every act to God and saw work as a way to experience the holiness of life.

The vision of holy work applies to everyone, whether in our daily employment, our education, or our volunteer work. Virtually all of us have "to pay the rent"—that is, we perform everyday tasks for ourselves and our families.

After my morning prayer and walk, the sun is still not risen; during this early-morning time, I have rotated writing with making coffee and putting laundry in the washing machine. Soon, I will help prepare my grandchildren for school. All these actions can be done as chores and encumbrances—or they can be done in the spirit of prayer, knowing that each of these everyday acts supports the people with whom I live and interact.

The shape of our employment is not always in our control. Certainly, peace of mind requires a sense of the Serenity Prayer, the recognition that our work depends on others for its success. But the spiritual and professional quality of our work also relies on our own self-awareness and willingness to dedicate our work to a higher cause and to change what we cannot accept, as activist Angela Davis counsels. In Hindu sages' quest for excellence, they counseled people to pursue what became known as Karma Yoga: Do your work well, dedicate it to the Divine, and let go of the ultimate results.

In this spiritual practice, I invite you to go through your day mindfully: first, in your imagination and then, by performing the necessary and helpful tasks that make up a glorious day. As the day begins, take time for silent reflection, asking God to reveal the holiness of your work and your encounters throughout the day. Consider your to-do list; think about the individuals you may meet in the day ahead. Devote each activity prayerfully to God, seeking in every encounter to bring beauty, wholeness, and compassion. In your daily activities, take a moment to focus on the holiness of each action.

For me, this means breathing and blessing. As I turned on the computer this morning, I took a few deep breaths, aligning myself and my writing with God's vision and pondering the impact of my work on my readers' spiritual lives. When I greet the store clerk at Giant in Bethesda, I will speak with friendship and respect and say a silent prayer for her well-being. When I return home to help prepare the grandchildren for school, I breathe deeply to help me respond to the chaos with joy and equanimity. I take a moment for a deep prayerful breath when I hear my cell phone ring.

I felt myself surrounded by the presence of God, and my soul was filled with joy.

—ANN LEE[62]

In addition, I invite you to simply stop every few hours for a minute to reflect on your current spiritual state and the course of your encounters. Have you experienced holiness or annoyance? Have you brought healing and beauty—or anxiety and conflict?

The ever-present God touches us each moment of the day, calling us toward wholeness through possibilities, insights, inspirations, synchronous encounters, and the wisdom of others. Are we awake and do we do our part to advance God's vision, "on earth as it is in heaven"?

Prayer of Awareness and Transformation

In every moment and every encounter
awaken me to your presence, Holy Mother.
Let me see traces of your love in every face
and inspiration in every action.
Let my ordinary tasks be done to give you glory
and bring beauty to the world you love.

8

BLACK ELK

Transformed by a Vision

Everywhere is the center of the world.
Everything is sacred.

—BLACK ELK

Mystical experiences can occur in moments of desperation in which our accustomed sense of security is shattered, and we experience both the grandeur and tragedy of life. American poet Theodore Roethke asserted that "in a dark time, the eye begins to see." Centuries earlier, John of the Cross described the "dark night of the soul" as the venue for spiritual transformation.

From behind prison walls, both the apostle Paul and Martin Luther King experienced unexpected freedom and penned some of the greatest spiritual literature of the

Western world. Persecuted by his fellow monks, John of the Cross discovered the light of Christ in the darkness of the dungeon. Appalled by the German church's support of the Third Reich, Dietrich Bonhoeffer discovered behind bars that only a suffering God can save humankind. In the turbulence of international conflict, United Nations General Secretary Dag Hammarskjold seized solitary moments for contemplation to reclaim his spiritual center. French philosopher, mystic, and activist Simone Weil's fragile health created a "thin place" through which she experienced her utter dependence on God's grace and was able to experience beauty amid suffering. The darkness can never quench the light of Divine inspiration.

Black Elk, destined by the Great Spirit, to be a *wicasa wakan*, an Oglala[63] holy man, spent his whole life witnessing the destruction of his people. Like Jesus of Nazareth, who experienced the oppressive violence of the Roman empire, Black Elk knew the pain of being powerless before the overwhelming power of America's belief in "manifest destiny." Disease, racism, military power, and cultural injustice decimated his people, the Oglala. As a child and throughout his early life, no doubt he heard slogans such as these: "The only good Indian is a dead Indian," and, "We must kill the Indian in the Indian."

White Americans, often with misguided messianic zeal, motivated by their belief in being a "chosen nation," not only sought to destroy the Indigenous nations but to also eliminate their culture and way of life. White settlers and religious leaders defined Indigenous people as "heathens" and saw them as having nothing of consequence to contribute to the dominant white culture. The spirituality of the Americas' First Nations people, rooted in their connection with the Earth, was inferior, whites believed, to faith in an all-powerful Judeo-Christian Deity, whose mighty hand had delivered the continent to his chosen Christian people.

In his lifetime, Black Elk saw powerful forces, motivated primarily by the racism and greed of Manifest Destiny, destroy his religion, culture, and way of life. Tragically, these same dynamics are still at work in American politics and economics.

Is not the sky a father and the earth a mother, and are not all living things with feet or wings or roots their children?

—BLACK ELK

Mystical experiences can emerge after years of preparation and commitment to spiritual practices. They also can burst forth with little or no warning, turning the world upside down for those to whom they come unbidden and sometimes unwanted.

Black Elk's Life

Although he was the son of an Oglala spiritual teacher and medicine man, Black Elk's childhood and adult visions come with little warning and initially with no preparation or choice on his part. The Great Spirit broke down the doors of his perception and revealed to him the infinite nature of its presence and the future of his people. Named *Kahnigapi*—"Chosen"—by his parents, Black Elk discovered that he was indeed chosen for a task: initially, to participate in the salvation of his people and later, as a village healer.

Born in what is today northeastern Wyoming during the "moon of the red cherries" (June or July) 1863, Black Elk began to hear voices at age four. At age five, with a storm on the horizon, he heard a voice coming from a cloud: "Listen! A voice is calling you." He saw two men coming toward him, singing a sacred song:

> *Behold, a sacred voice is calling you;*
> *All over the sky, a sacred voice is calling.*

Five years later, Black Elk had a Great Vision, intended, like the theophanies—God-encounters—of the biblical spiritual leaders Samuel and Isaiah, to bring wholeness to his people in a time of crisis. In the midst of eating a meal, Black Elk heard a voice, directed only to him: "It is time; now they are calling you."

Black Elk perceived himself, not unlike Isaiah in the Jerusalem Temple, being transported to the council of the Grandfathers, the divine beings who guide the Earth and most especially his own Oglala people. The Grandfathers gave Black Elk a vision and a teaching about his people's future path. He also received from the Grandfathers symbols of wisdom and healing to guide his life and his people through ritual enactment.

In words reminiscent of God's address to the Hebraic prophets, Black Elk heard: "My boy, have courage, for my power shall be yours, and you shall need it, for your nation on the earth will have great troubles." Black Elk saw first a vision of destruction and then a vision of hope for his people. Both death and life, he saw, were the Oglala nation's destiny:

> I was seeing in a sacred manner the shape of all things in the spirit, and the shape of all things as they must live together like one being. And I saw that the sacred hoop of my people was one of many hoops that made one circle, wide as daylight and as starlight, and in the center grew one mighty flowering tree to shelter all the children of one mother and one father. And I saw that it was holy.

Danger abounds, suffering will come, and the nation will be vanquished by invaders from the east. Yet, beyond the destruction, there is—like the apocalyptic visions of the Bible—a new creation, characterized by the unity of all peoples. We still wait for such a day!

It is from understanding that power comes . . . for nothing can live well except in a manner that is suited to the way the sacred Power of the World lives and moves.

—BLACK ELK

In his early twenties, Black Elk joined Buffalo Bill's Wild West Show and later Mexican Joe's carnival, traveling as a "showman" to France and England. He performed for Queen Victoria, whose kind words touched him. After three years abroad, Black Elk returned to the United States to find most of his people living on reservations. Their sacred rituals, such as the Sun Dance, had been banned. Medicine men and holy men had had to go underground, and their children were being assimilated into white culture. During this time, the emergence of the Ghost Dance, grounded in an apocalyptic vision of Indigenous renewal and the accompanying destruction of the white nation's power, gave the people a vision and hope for the future.

But this hope died with the massacre at Wounded Knee on December 29, 1890. Recalling the massacre, Black Elk lamented: "And I can see that something else died there in the bloody mud, and was buried in the blizzard. A people's dream died there. It was a beautiful dream."

For a time, Black Elk kept his visions to himself. Like the prophet Jeremiah, he worried that because of his age, none of the elders would pay attention to him. Still, the Great Vision called to him through his growing power. "Make haste!" the Great Spirit told him. "Before the day is out, something will happen."

Black Elk's anxiety grew. When he cried out for Divine help, he received this message: "It is time."

"Time for what?" Black Elk asked—and once again, he got an answer: "In a sacred manner you shall walk! Your nation shall behold you!"

Still, Black Elk waited, perhaps too long in his own estimation, to share his vision through religious rituals.

> I wondered when my power might grow, so that the rest might be as I had seen it in my vision. But I could say nothing about this to anyone, because I was only a boy and people would think I was foolish and say: "What can you do if even Sitting Bull can do nothing?"

Still, as the days went by, Black Elk's sensitivity to Divine messages grew. The nonhuman world—crows and coyotes—called out to him, "It is time! It is time." Black Robe, an aged medicine man, challenged him: "You must do your duty and perform this vision for your people on earth." Black Robe counselled him as Eli did young Samuel; Black Elk's own well-being and the well-being of his people, Black Robe believed, depended on the embodiment of the vision in rituals to inspire and strengthen the community.

The vision must be incarnated. It must take form among the people. When Black Elk performed his vision, the people felt new hope, and his own anxiety disappeared.

Visionary experiences are often initially private, as was Isaiah's encounter with God in the Jerusalem Temple—and yet many times, the Great Spirit intends them to be shared so they can convey the Divine vision to troubled humankind. The private becomes public to transform the world and give hope to the nation. This was the way of Moses, Samuel, Isaiah, and the apostles Peter and Paul, whose life-changing visions were meant not just for their own spiritual edification but for the healing and guidance of the Hebraic people and the expansion of the Gospel to all the world.

Often reluctantly, the prophet and shaman enter politics to bring their visions to empower a despairing people. Accordingly, Black Elk led the performance of the Horse Dance to cure himself and to bring hope to his people. He recalled after the performance of these sacred rituals: "Everything seemed good and beautiful now, and kind."

Not long after the ritual of the Horse Dance, Black Elk received another vision, calling him to a more public role in his community's spirituality. He began a healing ministry within his community. His visionary power enabled him to heal the sick—but despite his Great Vision, encounters with the Spirits, and vocation as a village healer, he could not heal the nation.

A few years after Wounded Knee, Black Elk settled down, married, and raised a family. His wife was an ardent Roman Catholic woman, and he was himself baptized as Nicholas Black Elk on the Feast of Saint Nicholas (December 6). Here is where the controversy about Black Elk emerges and the "historical" Black Elk becomes obscured. While I have followed John Neihardt's biography *Black Elk Speaks* in this book, several contemporary scholars critique Neihardt for downplaying Black Elk's Catholicism.[64] Black Elk became a Roman Catholic lay evangelist and catechist, bringing more than four hundred souls to Catholicism.

Reservation, church, and political authorities (white men) were pursuing a policy of "assimilation," marginalizing Indigenous rituals and spirituality and punishing school children for speaking their native languages. We now know that many missionary schools not only killed Indigenous children's spirits but also caused the deaths of hundreds, if not thousands, of them in both the United States and Canada. Even when these schools and policies no longer practiced physical violence, the process of genocide continued,

At the center of the universe dwells the Great Spirit. And that center is really everywhere. It is within each of us.

—BLACK ELK

albeit subtly, in the destruction of a people's spirituality and culture.

The Catholic Church nominated Black Elk for sainthood in 2016. Still, there is a good deal of controversy among Black Elk scholars about the relationship of his Catholicism to the Indigenous mysticism of his youth and young adulthood. Some historians believe Black Elk abandoned the Earth-based faith of his people for a few decades. Others believe he went underground with his visionary ministry to ensure his family's survival, while allowing him to make a good living working for the Catholic Church. Perhaps he was able to integrate Christianity with his already-existing beliefs.

According to historian Joe Jackson, Black Elk saw no fundamental difference between Catholicism and his Native mysticism. They pointed to the same reality, though with different languages and rituals. One of Black Elk's relatives said that unbeknownst to the Jesuit priests who employed him, Black Elk reinterpreted Christian doctrines and symbols in light of the Oglala worldview and their spiritual practices. In doing so, he overcame the dualism characteristic of Western Christianity. His nephew said that Black Elk:

> had decided that the Sioux religious way of life was pretty much the same as that of the Christian churches, and there was no reason to change what the Sioux were doing. We could pick up some Christian ways and teachings, and just work them in with our own, so that in the end both would be better.[65]

From this perspective, Black Elk was a pioneer in what is today described by terms such as hybrid spirituality, inter-spirituality, dual religious participation, or interspirituality—the integration of religious practices from different faith traditions into personal practice.

On the one hand, many committed Christians are active in their churches, regularly attend worship, and pray using the language of God and Jesus. On the other hand, these same Christians may practice—without feeling any spiritual or doctrinal dissonance—Zen Buddhist meditation; they may go on mindfulness retreats; promote personal well-being through yoga, Tai Chi, or reiki healing touch; dance in the spirit of Sufis; or participate in an Indigenous sweat lodge or prayers to the Four Corners. While we must be careful to respect the spiritual traditions of other religions, not claiming them as our own in a form of cultural appropriation, we can nevertheless learn much from other traditions to enhance our spiritual experiences. I believe that within and beneath every authentic spiritual tradition, the Divine Spirit moves and inspires, using many ways to nurture our spiritual growth as it's shaped by culture, ethnicity, and tradition.

> *It is the story of all life that is holy and good to tell, and of us two-leggeds sharing in it with the four-leggeds and the wings of the air and of green things; for these are children of one Mother and their father is one Spirit.*
>
> —BLACK ELK

Still, we must remember, as biographer Joe Jackson notes, Black Elk may have turned to Catholicism for purely practical reasons: "Because my children have to live in this world."[66] In their joining of Heaven and Earth, even mystics have to make pragmatic calculations. For Black Elk, this included the value of receiving from the Jesuits a house, free of charge, where he and his family could live safely.

Black Elk might have remained in obscurity had not poet, author, and ethnographer John Neihardt sought out the Oglala holy man. In 1930, in a series of interviews, Black Elk, now an old man, shared his vision and life story. He said he felt called to share his story with Neihardt to preserve it for future generations: "There is so much to teach you. What I know was given to me for all people, and it is true and it is beautiful. Soon I will be under the grass and it will be lost. You were sent to save it, and you must come back here so I can teach you."

Later, Joseph Epes Brown spoke with Black Elk about the sacred rituals of the Oglala people.[67] These texts gained popularity in the 1960s, not only as a result of growing pluralism and European Americans' recognition of Indigenous wisdom, but also in response to the growing self-affirmation among Indigenous peoples of their unique spirituality, culture, and political power.

Sight-impaired, Black Elk spent his last years on his family's farm, occasionally leading traditional dances and religious ceremonies. Like many of the eighth- and seventh-century BCE Hebraic prophets, Black Elk saw himself later in his life as a failure, a weak man who in his fallibility could not bring his Great Vision to Earth. Yet, despite his sense of failure, he did small things with compassion and brought healing and hope to many people in his community. God uses us all in ways we may never realize in this life.

Black Elk died in 1950, at the age of eighty-seven, a spirit person who had been given a Great Vision but who, like many spiritual visionaries before him, could not change the course of history for his people. Mystics are often unsuccessful in changing the pathways of nations, but their embodiment of God's Spirit, the Great Spirit, brings healing to their communities even as it inspires future spiritual adventures.

The Living Universe

Cultural and spiritual commentators have distinguished three ways of looking at our world.

- First is the way of enchantment, in which the universe is alive, humans are part of an intricate spiritual ecology, and God is present in the human and nonhuman worlds. From this perspective, every moment and every creature can be a revelation of God. God speaks through the breeze, thunderclouds, animal companions, and visionary experiences. All things are transparent in their revelation of Divinity.

- Second is the way of disenchantment, in which the nonhuman world is viewed as a senseless, valueless commodity to be used for human enrichment. Nature is opaque. If there is a God, Divinity's only purpose was to set the laws of Nature in motion and then retreat to the sidelines. When God does show up in this disenchanted world, it is through miraculous actions that violate the laws of Nature. Nature and the human body are machines to be manipulated for profit and power.

- Today, in light of human-kind's destruction of the ecosystem and negative impact on global climate patterns, many people are looking for a third way to respond to the world, a reenchantment of Nature and human existence. While not abandoning technology and science, spiritualities and economies of reenchantment proclaim:

Perhaps you have noticed that even in the very lightest breeze you can hear the voice of the cottonwood tree; this we understand is its prayer to the Great Spirit, for not only humans, but all things and all beings pray to the Spirit continually in differing ways.

—BLACK ELK

  ◦ the universality of experience and revelation in the nonhuman world;

  ◦ humankind as part of the part of the natural process and not alien to it;

  ◦ the intricate interdependence of life.

We hope to recover our spiritual roots, whatever they may be. The vision of the enchanted garden in which humankind and the nonhuman world live in harmony inspires us to perceive in a new way our relationship with the God "in whom we live and move and have our being" (Acts 17:28). We work to realize the corporate spirit of Shalom, the peaceable realm in which the world is transformed and renewed, and humans and nonhumans once again live together in harmony and joy.

Indigenous spirituality describes an enchanted universe, a living, interdependent world, in which all Creation reveals God's presence. The wisdom of enchantment inspires us to see the world in a sacred way, much like the psalmist who wrote that everything that breathes praises God (Psalm 148 and 150).

Sometimes dreams are wiser than waking.

—BLACK ELK

In describing the rituals of his people, Black Elk said:

We should understand well that all things are works of the Great Spirit. We should know that the Great Spirit is within all things: the trees, the rivers, the grasses, the mountains, and all four-legged animals, and the winged peoples; and even more important, we should understand that the Spirit is above all these things and peoples. When we do understand this deeply in our hearts, then we will fear, and know, and love the Great Spirit, and then we will be and act and live as the Great Spirit intends.[68]

Another Oglala visionary, Walking Buffalo, said: "We saw the Great Spirit's work in almost everything, sun, moon, trees, and mountains. Sometimes we approached him through these things."[69] What appeared to be idolatry to outsiders, blinded by their dualistic worldview and visions of Divine transcendence, was, in fact, the honoring of the

Great Spirit who is alive in every creature. Having forgotten the sacred spaces of their own tradition—Beth-El, the burning bush, Sinai, Galilee, Bethlehem—Christian missionaries could no longer see the holiness of place.

In contrast, in the dynamic depths of global mysticism and Indigenous experience, all things are sacred, including the daily tasks of childcare, cooking, and professional work. Everything is to be encountered in a sacred way. We are, as Moses discovered when he encountered a burning bush on his way to work, always on holy ground. Burning bushes are everywhere. Chimney rocks—hoodoos—turn our spirits toward the Divine. The flight of an eagle or the dive of an osprey awakens us to the Divine movements in our own lives.

It may be that some little root of the sacred tree still lives. Nourish it then, that it may leaf and bloom and fill with singing birds.

—BLACK ELK

In our quest for power and wealth, we have lost the simple experience of Divinity in everyday life. Entranced by our quest to control the nonhuman world, we have become alienated from the rhythms of revelation in earth, sea, sky, and land. Black Elk and indigenous holy people remind us that beneath our quests for domination, God is alive, challenging us to chart new pathways that honor the nonhuman world.

Nature is filled with Divinity and can communicate with us. The experience of the sacred is global, not just confined to humankind. Nature praises God, inviting us, in all our technological sophistication, to become companions with God and all Creation in healing the Earth.

Holy Visions

"Where there is no vision, the people perish," proclaims Proverbs 29:18 in the King James Version. God speaks through human beings to deliver messages of salvation for people and communities. The Great Spirit broke down the doors of perception and awakened Black Elk to the Infinite. Like young Samuel in the Hebrew scriptures, Black Elk as a child experienced God coming to him unexpectedly, overwhelming him with vision and vocation.

Holy visions testify to the permeability of the universe. God is not far off from any of us and can communicate a vision to a nine-year-old boy—or you and me. Each of us is a potential recipient of Divine wisdom, because the Great Spirit quietly inspires all Creation. God can transcend the boundary of Heaven and Earth, and give light to our world of darkness. The Divine Spirit is both ubiquitous—everywhere present—and uniquely omni-active, choosing to be present in some places and certain people with greater intensity than others. These are the "thin places," in which God reveals the Divine vision for us and the universe. Such moments enable us, as Black Elk testified, to see in a sacred way.

While Black Elk's visions initially came unbidden, many of his contemporaries—and Black Elk himself later in life—prepared to discern God's presence by "crying for a vision." This practice involved prayerful preparation through purifying ceremonies and times of retreat from everyday life.

Vision quests, much like Thoreau's wilderness sauntering and Jesus' retreat in the wilderness, enable us to hear

God's voice, once our society's many voices have stilled. Religion involves solitariness—but for Black Elk, the Hebraic prophets, Indigenous vision questers, and Jesus of Nazareth, solitude drives us back into the chaos of daily life. Inspired by their visions, Black Elk, the prophets, and Jesus discovered that their vocation was relational, intended to embody God's vision of a transformed and healthy social order, "on earth as it is in heaven."

> *All things are our relatives; what we do to everything, we do to ourselves. All is really One.*
>
> —BLACK ELK

The Power of Ritual

In a time of national uncertainty, crying for his own vision, the mysterious prophet Habakkuk received a word from God:

> I will stand at my watch post, and station myself on the rampart; I will keep watch to see what he will say to me, and what he will answer concerning my complaint. Then [Yahweh] answered me and said: Write the vision; make it plain on tablets, so that a runner may read it. For there is still a vision for the appointed time; it speaks of the end, and does not lie. If it seems to tarry, wait for it; it will surely come, it will not delay. (2:1–3)

While heavenly in origin, the products of Divine inspiration, visions gain power when they are shared with others. What begins privately comes alive in public presentation.

Divine guidance takes flesh in words and actions to transform the social order. As God said to Habakkuk, "Write the vision; make it plain on tablets," so it can shape the larger community.

Black Elk admits that "a man who has a vision is not able to use the power of it until after he has performed the vision on earth for people to see." After performing the dog vision, Black Elk claimed his role as a healer or medicine man. Performing the vision unlocked new energies that flowed through him to bring healing to the anxious and diseased:

> I cured with the power that came through me. Of course it was not I who cured. It was the power from the outer world, and the visions and ceremonies had only made me like a hole through which power could come to the two leggeds. If I thought I was doing it myself, the hole would close up and no power would flow through me.

Black Elk's integration of vision, performance, and healing reminds me of my experience with reiki healing touch. With each new

The first peace, which is the most important, is that which comes within the souls of people when they realize their relationship, their oneness with the universe and all its powers, and when they realize that at the center of the universe dwells the Great Spirit, and that this center is really everywhere, it is within each of us.

—BLACK ELK[70]

initiation from level one to the master level, the initiation rituals enhanced the flow of energy in my cells and spirit. Sharing that energy through reiki treatments and my own practice as a reiki master-teacher initiating others through the reiki rituals deepened and intensified my sense of healing energy.

In the intricate and interdependent ecology of Spirit, we are inspired as we inspire others, comforted as we comfort others, and healed as we heal others. Black Elk could not save his people, but sharing his visionary experiences brought healing and hope in a troubled time—and his words can continue to teach us today.

Given America's dark history, today's mystics must call the United States to confess the sin of genocide—along with all the other sins rooted in racism—and explore ways to "repair the world" (*tikkun olam*, according to Jewish tradition) by working with Indigenous communities in the areas of economics, health, and education

Seeing the World in a Holy Way

American poet Walt Whitman asserted that all is miracle, and Rabbi Abraham Joshua Heschel proclaimed that the heart of religious experience is radical amazement. While we cannot control visionary and ecstatic experiences, we can awaken to holiness and wonder in our midst. The spiritual adventure involves pausing long enough to notice the holiness of the world around us.

We can see the world as dull, lifeless, intended to be a commodity for pleasure and consumption. Or we can train our eyes to see beauty. We can, with Heschel, "ask for wonder." In a similar fashion, Indigenous peoples speak of "crying for a vision," that is, asking for deeper knowledge of themselves, their vocation, and the world around them. Black Elk invites us to experience a re-enchanted universe in which each moment and every encounter is a window into Divinity. He speaks of walking in a sacred manner.

And so, in this exercise, awaken your senses to wonder. Become "all sense" as you breathe in the world's beauty. Pause to notice and open yourself to holiness in every situation. Let go of your need—for just this moment—to be somewhere else than in this Holy Here-and-Now. Experience the wonder of your body, your emotional life, your creativity, and the plants, animals, land, air, and water around you. Let your openness to beauty awaken you to a life of praise and gratitude.

Let every step you take upon the earth be as a prayer.

—BLACK ELK

Prayer of Our Spiritual Home

With beauty all around me, I walk.
With sacred steps, I open
to the glorious universe around me.
With senses open, I rejoice
in the wonder of all being
and the wonder of my being.
I give thanks for all good gifts
and share beauty wherever I walk.

9

JOHN MUIR

The Holiness of Beauty

I'd rather be in the mountains thinking of God,
than in church thinking about the mountains.

—JOHN MUIR

Philosopher Alfred North Whitehead asserted that the universe's aim is toward the production of beauty. According to Whitehead, beauty not only nurtures our spirits; it is also embedded in the very nature of reality. Beauty is grounded in God's vision for each person and all Creation. The orderly movements of the stars, the growth of flora and fauna, the breaching whale, the perusing pangolin, the human face, the wildness of the sea, and the majestic redwoods all reveal God's creative artistry. God is the poet of the universe, guiding the world with the Divine vision of truth, goodness, and beauty. As breathtaking as human artistry and creativity may be, human inventiveness is lured forward by dramatic natural vistas, uncharted frontiers, and infinite horizons.

Yet beauty is fragile. With the advent of global climate change, seashores, forests, and animal species are in peril. Our children and grandchildren are at risk, as well as coastal cities. Human decisions have put some of the world's most sacred spaces in danger. Beauty enriches our spiritual lives and inspires creativity at every level of existence—but beauty is easily defaced by thoughtless humans, hell-bent on consumption and profit-making. Shouts of "drill, baby, drill!" drown out the songs of the humpbacked whales and the melodies of songbirds.

To counteract this destructive reality, the preservation of sacred spaces becomes both a religious and ethical mandate. Wilderness lands open us to new horizons and inspire new frontiers in the human adventure.

The Life of John Muir

John Muir (1838–2014) had a vision of beauty that called him to become (with President Theodore Roosevelt) the parent of the U.S. national parks system and the founder of the Sierra Club. Reflecting on the necessity of national parks such as his beloved Yosemite, Muir said: "There is love of wild nature in everybody . . . an anxious mother-love ever showing itself whether recognized or no, and however covered by cares or duties." Furthermore, he said, "In God's wildness lies the hope of the world, —the great, fresh, unblighted unredeemed wilderness."[71] Following in the footsteps of Thoreau, Muir justified the establishment of national parks in the following affirmation: "Everybody needs beauty as well as bread, places to play in and pray in where Nature may heal and cheer and give strength to body and soul alike."[72]

Climb the mountains and get their good tidings. Nature's peace will flow into you as sunshine flows into trees. The winds will blow their own freshness into you, and the storms their energy, while care will drop away from you like the leaves of Autumn.

—JOHN MUIR[73]

Muir was a Nature mystic who experienced God in streams, woodlands, skies, and vistas more than in church sanctuaries and basilicas. His cathedral was Nature, not the brick-and-mortar creations of human artifice. Muir was truly "cosmopolitan"—that is, a citizen of the cosmos. He was part of Nature, and Nature flowed through him.

John Muir's life joined industry and piety, inventiveness and wonder. Born in Scotland, the son of a shopkeeper, Muir emigrated to the United States with his family at age eleven. His father, Daniel Muir, a member of a Scots nonconformist religious sect, sought the wide horizons of America to follow his faith, find freedom from lifeless tradition, and seek financial prosperity by becoming a Wisconsin farmer. He finally succeeded, through hard work and canny business practices, in becoming a large and prosperous landowner.

His work ethic extended to his children. Young John Muir, age twelve, worked as many as sixteen hours a day, six days a week. After becoming a member of the Disciples of

Christ, an American religious movement, Daniel Muir sought to inculcate his children in biblical wisdom, simple piety, sabbath-keeping, and hard work. Though he suffered from what his son John would call "the vice of over industry," Daniel Muir also encouraged his children to experience Divine glory in the wonders of God's handiwork—the stars and the natural world.[74]

The love of Nature was built into John Muir's spiritual DNA. Not content with a career in farming, young John turned to his great love: science and the study of Nature. He regularly awakened at 1:00 a.m. to pursue his studies before a long workday. He hiked the hills and vales, experiencing his unity with crag and meadow, flora and fauna. His youthful encounters with the Nature mysticism of poets Robert Burns and William Wordsworth shaped his vision of Nature as an interdependent, large-souled community of communities.

When one tugs at a single thing in nature, they find it attached to the rest of the world.

–JOHN MUIR

In his early twenties, Muir left home to promote his inventions—mostly labor-saving devices—and then enrolled in the University of Wisconsin. Although he eventually abandoned the University of Wisconsin for studies at what he described as the University of Nature, Muir joined human creativity, embodied in his creation of innovative devices, with a sense of the awesomeness of the untouched wilderness. Throughout his life, he sought to integrate industrial progress with the protection of Nature.

Muir tramped from Wisconsin to Ontario, where he worked at a sawmill and designed more efficient mill equipment. When the mill burned down, Muir found work at an Indianapolis carriage factory, where an industrial accident left him temporarily blind. When Muir's eyesight returned, he committed himself to seeing beauty everywhere and embarked on a trek to Florida, where he contracted near-fatal malaria.

When Muir recovered, he abandoned business in favor of wanderlust. "I bid adieu to mechanical inventions," Muir wrote in his journal, "determined to devote the rest of my life to the study of the inventions of God." At thirty, Muir sailed to California and hiked from San Francisco to Yosemite, where he discovered his sacred place, the thin place where God spoke to him through mountains, wind, animal companions, and wild weather. Ten years later, he began to make a name for himself as a naturalist and Nature writer. He guided Ralph Waldo Emerson around Yosemite, and Emerson described Muir as one of his men, similar in spirit to the Transcendentalist philosopher-mystic.

At forty-two, Muir married Louise Strentzel, the daughter of a wealthy farmer and orchardist. For the next several years, Muir devoted himself to managing and expanding his father-in-law's holdings, even commissioning a railroad stop adjacent to the family property. The lure of Nature still inspired the prosperous farmer, husband, and father, and from time to time, he went on extended expeditions to Alaska and his beloved Yosemite. In his fifties, a successful businessperson and writer, Muir was invited to become a founder and first president of the Sierra Club, whose mission was to preserve the wilderness as a sanctuary for the spirit.

In his leadership of the Sierra Club, Muir had the opportunity in 1906 to accompany President Theodore Roosevelt on a hike through Yosemite. The two men become close friends and collaborators in the national park movement. In the following decades, Muir devoted himself to preserving the wilderness as a place of inspiration, recreation, refreshment, and piety.

For Muir, the untamed wilderness is the final horizon for the American spirit; its preservation, even at the cost of profit and progress, is essential to building our nation's character. For the remainder of his life—he died at age seventy-six—Muir pursued writing, while he regularly bathed his spirit in the wonder and wildness of the untamed wilderness.

> *Between every two pine trees there is a door leading to a new way of life.*
>
> —JOHN MUIR

Nature as the Temple of God

The apostle Paul spoke of the body as the temple of God, a shrine reflecting God's wisdom and care. Muir would have affirmed Paul's body spirituality, but he would have gone beyond the apostle to proclaim that the entire world is the body of God, and that humankind is embedded in the nonhuman world of Nature. Muir exclaimed in his journal: "Wonderful, how completely everything in wild Nature fits into us, as if truly part and parent of us. . . . The sun shines not on us but in us. . . . The trees wave and the flowers bloom in our bodies as well as our souls." According to editor Tim Flinders, Muir believed that "Yosemite Valley was a *sanctum sanctorum* [holy of holies] . . . a divine manuscript as revelatory of the divine as the Bible itself." Moreover, "every natural object is a conductor of Divinity and only by coming into contact with them . . . may we be filled with the Holy Ghost."

John Muir used his physical senses to embrace the Spirit in the wonders of Nature. He saw Nature—all Nature, including humankind—as enchanted, despite the impact of human industry and greed. Hidden by our avarice and materialism, God is nevertheless still speaking in our lives: in the cells of our bodies, the breath we take, the beating of our hearts, and moments of insight and intuition. We are always connected with the nonhuman world, even when we attempt to create human environments independent of the variable seasons and weather patterns of Nature. "Rocks and waters," wrote Muir, "are words of God and so are humans. We all flow from one fountain soul. All are expressions of one Love."

We are one with the nonhuman world. The energy of love flows through and gives life to all things. In bathing our spirits in the beauties of Nature, we discover not only our kinship with all Creation; we also discover our true selves. Muir described his personal sense of the Holy Here-and-Now: "I only went out for a walk, and finally concluded to stay out till sundown, for going out I found was really going in."

"Going out" into Nature is "really going in" to the Spirit, because all life is graced with God's presence. All Creation manifests God's wisdom. As the Gospel of Thomas proclaims:

Jesus says: "I am the light which is on them all. I am the All, and the All has gone out from me and the All has come back to me. Cleave the wood: I am there; lift the stone and thou shalt find me there!" (Saying 77)

Echoing Jesus' words, Muir noted, "All of the individual 'things' or 'beings' into which the world is wrought are sparks of the Divine Soul variously clothed upon with flesh, leaves, or that harder tissue called rock." Furthermore, he said, "The whole wilderness seems to be alive and familiar, full of humanity. . . . The very stones seem talkative, sympathetic, brotherly. No wonder we consider that we all have the same father and mother." God's wisdom guides every creature: "Every particle of rock or water or air has God by its side leading it the way it should go. How else would it know where to go or what to do?"

God creates out of joy and love. The Word made flesh is incarnate in our flesh and blood, in the few right whales still swimming the seas,[75] in the endangered pangolin sought for medicinal purposes and gourmet delights, in the polar bear leaping from one patch of ice to another looking for solid ground, and in the soaring eagle that inspires us to fly high ourselves. It is, as Muir wrote to a friend, a "blessed thing to go free in the light of this beautiful world, to see God playing on everything as a [person] would play on an instrument."

> *All the wild world is beautiful, and it matters but little where we go . . . everywhere and always we are in God's eternal beauty and love.*
>
> —JOHN MUIR[76]

Spirituality of the Senses

Mystics and theologians have disagreed about how we best know the Divine. The apophatic way, as we discussed earlier, sees God as a deep mystery, beyond human comprehension. God is the dark night and the deep darkness that defies human imagery. The kataphatic way—the way of imagery—celebrates God's presence in the physical world perceived by the senses. God is not limited to any expression in the world, but the world reveals God's nature in the same way our bodies reveal our spirits. In the same spirit as the psalmist, Muir described the holiness of a Yosemite morning: "This is the morning of creation! The whole thing is beginning now! The mountains are singing together."

Following the lead of Moses on Sinai, Muir advocated a mountaintop spirituality; he counseled: "Get up into the mountains and get close to God." The wilderness is a "Divine manuscript," "opening a thousand windows to show us God," for "rocks and waters are words of God. . . . We all flow from one fountain Soul. All are expressions of Love." The "hospitable, Godful wilderness" is food for our souls and inspiration for our spiritual adventures. God is also beyond our particular sacred spaces, but Yosemite's mountains and meadows, the rolling waves, the breaching whale, a starry, starry night, evoke the Divine in us because they are divine themselves. All eye or all sense, we see God's face, hear God's voice, touch God's skin, taste God's bounty, and smell God's presence.

The wilderness beckoned Muir beyond time and space to experience Divinity in the Holy Here-and-Now. "I don't know anything of time, and very little of space. . . . I have spent every Sabbath for the last two months in the spirit world . . . in unselected atmospheres of terrestrial glory diffused evenly throughout my whole substance."

Wildness and Responsibility

If the Divinely guided aim of the universe is toward the production of beauty, as Whitehead asserted, then our experiences of beauty must inspire us to protect and nurture beauty everywhere. Although Muir believed in the American vision of progress, he also recognized that human desire and consumption should not lead to the destruction of natural habitats, woodlands, ponds, and wilderness places.

When we contemplate the whole globe as one great dewdrop, striped and dotted with continents and islands, flying through space with other stars all singing and shining together as one, the whole universe appears as an infinite storm of beauty.

—JOHN MUIR

Muir also affirmed that nonhuman lives have value and importance apart from human interest. Every creature plays a role in the evolving universe. Every creature, even those we scorn—ticks, mosquitos, great white sharks, and cobras, for instance—plays a role in the intricate ecology of Divine creativity. As our companions in the holiness of beauty, nonhumans have rights that must be considered in our economic and lifestyle decisions.

The loss of species and the destruction of forests, meadows, jungles, and bodies of water are moral and spiritual issues. According to author Tim Flinders, "Muir argued that every being had been created for itself, rather than to serve 'Lord Man.'" Muir denounced anthropocentric worldviews that place Nature entirely at our disposal. "How narrow we, selfish, conceited creatures are in our sympathies! How blind to the rights of all the rest of creation." Jesus also loved the birds of the air and lilies of the field as revelations of Divine artistry not products for human consumption. He reveled in the nonhuman world and the world of children, as God's glory embodied in space and time.

For Muir, the establishment of national parks and Nature preserves was a moral and spiritual issue, essential to human evolution. Humankind, he believed, needs the spiritual vistas, refreshment, and inspiration of wilderness to flourish. Muir's advocacy for a national park system was grounded in his recognition that wild places transform the human soul. In wildness, our spirits expand as we grow in wisdom and stature.

The battle for conservation will go on endlessly. It is part of the universal battle between right and wrong.

–JOHN MUIR

Back to Nature

Today, there are only a handful of truly wilderness spots, untouched by humankind, on the North American continent. Still, John Muir's mystic vision invites us to go back to Nature, to seek out the nonhuman world as a revelation of God's Spirit.

In virtually every metropolitan area, there are oases of quiet beauty. When I spent a year living in a high-rise in

Chevy Chase, Maryland, just a block from Wisconsin Avenue, one of the most traveled thoroughfares in the Washington, DC, area, I found a place of solitude just a few hundred yards from my apartment. I called this wooded glade and the stream that flowed through it the "One Aker Wood," in a play on Winnie the Pooh's "Hundred Aker Wood." My toddler grandson and I sat by the stream, hearing the song of flowing waters. We followed the path of butterflies and listened to the songbirds.

North America's national parks or secluded seashores can be catalysts for spiritual pilgrimages. You may also find inspiration from Nature documentaries on PBS and the National Geographic channels. To experience Muir's legacy, I invite you to view Ken Burn's *National Parks: America's Best Idea.*

As part of your spiritual practice, seek out experiences of beauty near and far. Navajo spiritual guides assert: "With beauty all around me I walk." Wherever we are, we are surrounded by beauty, and awakening to beauty can transform our lives. In gratitude for the beauty of the Earth, consider supporting—financially, politically, or by your direct involvement—one of the many environmental justice groups, such as the Audubon Society, Greenpeace, Environmental Defense Fund, 350.org, or the Sierra Club.

In God's wildness lies the hope of the world.

—JOHN MUIR

Prayer of Our Spiritual Home

With beauty all around, let me walk.
Let all my senses be bathed in beauty
as I give thanks for all Creation.
Let me revel, Creator, in your Infinity and Love.
Let every breath praise you
and bring healing to the Earth.

JOHN MUIR

10

HOWARD THURMAN

Contemplative Activism

Don't ask what the world needs.
Ask what makes you come alive and go do it.
Because what the world needs is more people
who have come alive.

—HOWARD THURMAN[77]

Mystics are often accused of being so spiritual that they are of no use in the real world of work and relationships. With eyes fixed on eternity, the world of politics and economics may seem irrelevant to their spiritual journeys. Yet, while some mystics turn from the hardscrabble world of social involvement, others are driven into the world in response to their encounters with the Holy.

Many mystics discover the presence of God embedded in the challenges of daily life and political involvement. In a mystic vision, Isaiah heard God's call: "Whom shall I send and who will go for us?" In response, he stammered, "Here I am, send me," knowing that from now on his mission was to speak Divine justice to a wayward people and their equally wayward leaders. Dorothy Day discovered that in feeding the poor she experienced the same spiritual fervor as she did when sharing Christ's body and blood at communion. Isolated from the world in a Trappist monastery, Thomas Merton understood that he too is a "guilty bystander," who needed confront the evils of the nuclear arms race and American imperialism. Mystics realize that God loves the world—this flesh-and-blood, cellulose-and-chlorophyll world—and faithfulness to their mystical visions requires that they participate in the Earth's healing.

Some mystics' spiritual growth emerges amid the toxicity of racism, sexism, and political oppression. With their backs against the wall, marginalized and demeaned by oppression, their mystical visions are an implicit affirmation of their value as God's beloved children—and a protest against anything that stands in the way of people achieving their full humanity as God's children.

Howard Thurman's Life

The grandson of an enslaved woman, Howard Thurman (1899-1981) grew up in segregated Daytona Beach, Florida. Daily, he experienced the implicit and explicit violence of Jim Crow regulations and white supremacist groups. He experienced firsthand the dangers of "driving while Black," and despite his later professional successes, he found himself and his family often relegated to second-class status.

Against the odds, young Howard Thurman attended Morehouse College and Rochester Theological Seminary; he then launched a successful professional career as a professor, dean, and chaplain at various well-respected universities. He was a spiritual mentor to Martin Luther King Jr., who often carried in his briefcase Thurman's classic in liberation theology, *Jesus and the Disinherited.*

As a pastor, preacher, and professor, Thurman aspired to nurture a "friendly world of friendly people," even amid the racial polarization of his time. Recognized as one of North America's most influential preachers, Thurman joined poetry, ritual, silence, spiritual exercises, and preaching in the worship services he led. He also invited the worshipping community to experience God's presence in his poetry. Authentic spirituality makes music in the heart. It dismantles everything in our personal, political, and economic lives that blocks people from experiencing their full humanity as God's beloved children.

Howard Thurman is one of my spiritual and theological mentors. I met him first in the early 1970s when he gave a talk at my college church, Grace Baptist Church in San Jose, California, where his quiet integration of spirituality and peacemaking entranced me. At the height of the Vietnam War, his words helped me find creative ways to respond nonviolently to our nation's unjust war. A few years later, I encountered Thurman once again when I was a graduate student at Claremont Graduate School, where I heard him speak again on the importance of integrating spirituality and social transformation. His "affirmative mysticism" (to use a term from one of his mentors, Quaker Rufus Jones) inspired me.

Mystics, Thurman believed, must translate their solitary meditations into real-world strategies to resolve social injustice and violence. His guidance has become even more significant to me in the past few years, as I have recognized my responsibility to confront racism, environmental destruction, and the rising incivility in the United States—while maintaining my spiritual connection with people whose behaviors and positions I challenge.[78]

Unity Within Diversity

Although he lived in a profoundly divided America where he faced racism daily, Thurman saw the world as a dynamic and interdependent whole, where there is no "other." We are one in God's Spirit. A primeval wholeness undergirds and challenges the brutality of racial and ethnic division.

As a child, Thurman had already experienced the profound unity with all Creation that inspired him throughout his life:

> I could sit my back against its trunk, and feel the same peace that would come to me at night. I could reach down in the quiet places of the spirit, take out my bruises and my joys, unfold them, and talk about them. I could talk aloud to the oak tree and know that I was understood. It, too, was part of my reality,

like the woods, the night, and the pounding surf, my earliest companions, giving me space.[79]

He experienced the universe as one great pulse of Divine Love.

Growing up, he felt at one with the winds and sea. "When I was young," Thurman recalled, "I found more companionship in Nature than with people. . . . The quiet, even the danger, of the woods provided my rather lonely spirit with a sense of belonging that did not depend on human relationships."[80] He learned that God is the Holy Here-and-Now, whispering in the winds, energizing our heartbeats, and meeting us as the deepest reality of every encounter. Thurman affirmed that "all things were one lung through which all life breathed . . . a vast rhythm enveloping all, but I was a part of it and it was a part of me."[81]

While Thurman experienced the ambiguity of organized religion and the narrowness of its binary saved-versus-unsaved theology, he was always thankful for the love he received in his childhood congregation, proving to him that God is larger than an institution. Revelation is global and touches every person and faith tradition. Churches may exclude based on doctrine and ritual, but God embraces all. In spite of the imperfections of religious institutions, Thurman, as a child and throughout his lifetime, leaned on a Personal Reality that was both infinite and intimate.

An event from his childhood, the appearance of Halley's Comet in 1910, typifies Thurman's lifelong sense of Divine Providence moving in and through all things. News of the comet elicited apocalyptic fears in Howard's neighborhood, and some of his neighbors even purchased "comet pills" to protect them when the comet struck the Earth. A frightened eleven-year-old Thurman asked his mother, "What will happen to us if that thing falls from out of the sky?"

With a sense of peace that transformed fear into trust, she responded, "Nothing will happen to us, Howard. God will take care of us."[82] In life and death, in peace and conflict, Thurman discovered that God is with us, sustaining and guiding our personal adventures. Even in times of profound upheaval, we can with the psalmist "be still" and know that God is with us (Psalm 46:10).

Jacob's ladder of angels begins on Earth, in ordinary life, and reaches upward, connecting us with Heaven. In a similar way, Thurman's mystic vision embraced the Earth in all its beauty. The beauty of Nature and our kinship with flora and fauna inspired him to see God in all things and all things in God. He was united with all humanity, despite its diversities of belief, ethnicity, race, politics, and sexuality. God is in this place—every place—and Thurman, like other mystics despite their limitations and finitude, experienced life as being filled with Divinity.

Mystics as Social Reformers

Thurman's mysticism was both practical and spiritual. If we follow his example, our encounters with the Divine will impel us into the hardscrabble world of political involvement and justice-seeking. God speaks to prophets and gives them a mission

In looking at his own spiritual journey as a Black American subject to the realities of racism, Thurman wrote:

> I have sought a way of life that could come under the influence of, and be informed by, the fruits of the inner life. The cruel vicissitudes of the social situation in which I have been forced to live in American society have made it vital for me to seek resources, or a resource to which I could have access as I sought means for sustaining the personal enterprise of my life beyond all the ravages inflicted upon it by the brutalities of the social order.[83]

Mysticism is always historical and contextual. Mystics must deal with the challenges of their particular social location. Thurman recognized that he, along with other people of color in a racist society, was "an outsider in the community of power," someone who had to struggle daily to affirm his identity and find his place in a society whose structures often disregarded his voice and value.[84]

Thurman's only hope for self-transcendence was to "find within myself the door that no [one] could shut, to locate resources that are uniquely mine, to which I must be true if the personal enterprise of my life is to be sustained despite the ravages inflicted upon it by society."[85] His personal path enabled him "to be strong enough to carry the heavy stones of the spirit which are necessary for the foundations of the kingdom of friendly [people] underneath a friendly sky."[86]

In a lecture given a few years before his death, Thurman defined mysticism "as the response of the individual to a personal encounter with God within [their] own soul. This is my working definition. Such a response is total, affecting the inner quality of the life and its outward expression as its manifestation."[87] In the solitude of prayer, the mystic experiences unity with humankind in all its diversity and recognizes the power of institutions to support or oppose the well-being of humanity. The mystic challenges everything that stands between encounters with the Holy One, much of which is the result of injustice, racism, and exploitation. The mystic descends—or is it an ascension?—from the mountaintop to the maelstrom to bring healing to the Earth and its peoples. "Social action," wrote Thurman, "is an expression of resistance against whatever tends to, or separates one, from the experience of God, who is the ground of [their] being."[88]

Social action to liberate human possibility is necessary when our experiences with God have led us to discover the movement of Divinity in all Creation. As Thurman wrote:

> For the mystic, social action is sacramental, because it is not an end in itself. Always, it is the individual who must be addressed, located, and released, underneath [their] misery and [their] hunger and [their] destitution. That whatever may be blocking [their] way to [their] own center where[their] altar may be found, this must be removed."[89]

In the spirit of the Hebraic prophets, the mystic is concerned about the spiritual lives of the oppressor as well as the oppressed, for the oppressor may have gained the world but lost their soul in the process. Oppression, as the Hebraic prophet Amos proclaimed, creates among the oppressors a spiritual famine, since they cannot hear God's voice. The prophetic mystic, like a surgeon, may inflict pain to achieve the long-term healing of people and institutions.

This may involve, as it did in the Civil Rights, Black Lives Matter, and the Me-Too movements, protests against government policies. It inspires picketing as well as prayer. Protest and boycott agitate the comfortable so the oppressed may experience comfort. Thurman wrote:

> What is important for the mystic is that the purpose of the shock treatment is to hold before the offender a mirror that registers an image of [themselves], that reflects the image of those who suffer at [their] hands. The total function of such action is to tear [people] from any alignments that prevent them from putting themselves in the other person's place, but it must never be forgotten that the central concern of the mystic is to seek to remove anything that prevents the individual from free and easy access to [their] own altar-stair that is in [their] own heart.[90]

In an interdependent world, we are all connected. Salvation is communal and holistic; it must include both the oppressor and the oppressed.

If the spirit of the United States is to be healed in this time of rising white nationalism, hate crimes against people of color, incivility, and the undermining of democracy, then our nation needs prophetic healing. We need to be activists like Howard Thurman, grounded in solidarity with all Creation and love for both the those who are oppressed and those who perpetrate the evils we deplore.

Prophetic Healing

Thurman believed Jesus' message of loving hospitality is especially profound because Jesus spent his entire life in an occupied nation. Jesus spoke to people who had no power and who were totally at the mercy of the oppressor's whims.

Do not be silent; there is no limit to the power that may be released through you.

—HOWARD THURMAN[91]

In Thurman's reflections on poverty and racism, he asserted that one of the greatest evils of marginalization and oppression is the stunting of children's imaginations. We are meant to soar, but oppression and poverty plant us firmly in a world of pain. It stunts our ability to imagine a different reality that reflects the Realm of God.

Mysticism, when it's grounded in the unity of all Creation and the redeemability of those who oppress, leads to prophetic healing, challenging oppression. The oppressor must be forcefully confronted to liberate the oppressed from spiritual and physical bondage, but confrontation is inspired by hopeful reconciliation, the type of reconciliation we have seen in the work of Mahatma Gandhi, Desmond Tutu, and Nelson Mandela.

This prophetic healing, inspired by mysticism, begins with the quest for common ground, a place where our embrace of diversity brings us toward unity. Thurman wrote:

> The place where imagination shows its greatest power as the agent of God is in the miracle which it creates, when one person, standing where they are, is able, while remaining there, to put themselves in another's place.[92]

The quest for common ground requires the affirmation that all people "belong to each other," and people who shut themselves away from others diminish themselves.[93] Mystics create bridges between apathy and empathy. The unity they experience breaks down the walls of separation and enlarges them to embrace other people's experiences as their own. They live by Jesus' counsel to "love your neighbor as yourself."

Whatever may be the tensions and the stresses of a particular day, there is always lurking close at hand the trailing beauty of forgotten joy or unremembered peace.

—HOWARD THURMAN[94]

This liberating mysticism joins us with others and enables us to hold in creative tension protest and prayer, challenge and compassion. Thurman wrote:

> As prophets of the Most High God, it is your divine assignment to announce that [humanity] lives [their] days under the persistent scrutiny of God—that God

is at stake in a [human being's] day. . . . You must live and proclaim a faith that will make [people] affirm themselves and their fellow [humans] as children of God. You must lay your lives on the altar of social change so that wherever you are the Kingdom of God is at hand.[95]

When we see holiness everywhere and seek to liberate the divine within both the oppressed and the oppressors, God's realm comes here and now, in our world of struggle.

In a time when most of us feel powerless to bring about meaningful change, the mystic lives by the affirmation that the world is saved by one encounter and action at a time. We too can become catalysts for creative transformation in our communities and political institutions, as we become God's companions in healing the Earth.

Our recognition of our complicity in systemic injustice, grounded in our privilege, inspires us to join God's quest for healing the Earth and its people. Thurman wrote:

It is urgent to hold steadily in the mind the utter responsibility of the solitary individual to do everything with all [their] heart and mind to arrest the development of the consequence of private and personal evil resulting from the interaction of the impersonal forces that surround us. To cancel out between you and another all personal and private evil, to put your life squarely on the side of the good thing because it is good, and for no other reason, is to anticipate the Kingdom of God at the level of your functioning.[96]

Healing the World
One Moment at a Time

Rabbi Hillel the Elder, whose wisdom may have influenced Jesus, gave the following counsel for spiritual seekers: "If I am not for myself, who will be? But if I am only for myself, who am I? If not now, when?"

If we are to achieve Thurman and King's dream of the Beloved Community, we need to see each encounter as holy. We need to be wide-awake—"woke"—people, who join our experiences of God with empathy for those who experience injustice.

In the spirit of Hillel, you might ask yourself the following questions:

- *Am I for myself?* Do I attend to my spiritual life and personal well-being?" Mystics cultivate the divine center in their own lives, bodies, minds, and spirits. In loving your neighbor, do you also love yourself? In an interdependent world, healthy self-care and spiritual commitment nurture the well-being of others and enable us to be patient with the slow progress of human history. Moreover, commitment to prayer and self-care is the greatest antidote to compassion fatigue (burnout) in our quest to build the Realm of Heaven. Make a commitment to nurture your body, mind, spirit, and relationships.

- *Am I only for myself?* Am I primarily concerned with my happiness and my nation's security at the expense of other people's well-being? Thurman, along with

Hillel, realized that personal health and well-being require healthy communities and governmental structures. Do I reach out to others with empathy and support? Do I see their happiness as crucial to my own? Do I care for my nation's domestic and foreign policies as they relate to the planet's most vulnerable people and species? Do I look beyond my lifetime as an individual and citizen to secure the well-being of future generations?

- *If not now, when?* What one action and commitment can I make today—to promote my own spiritual well-being, to increase the well-being of those with whom I daily interact, and to support justice and hospitality in my land? A great journey begins with a first—and often small—step. "This is the day that God has made," proclaimed the psalmist—and on *this* day, let me rejoice, let me pray, let me seek justice and healing.

There is something in every one of you that waits and listens for the sound of the genuine in yourself. It is the only true guide you will ever have. And if you cannot hear it, you will all of your life spend your days on the ends of strings that somebody else pulls.

—HOWARD THURMAN[97]

Take a few minutes to discern your calling for today. Then put it into practice, even if only in a small way.

Prayer of Our Spiritual Home

In this holy moment,
let me commit myself to justice.
In this wondrous now,
let me reach out in love and care.
This is the day God has given me.
Let me live it in delight, wonder,
service, and care.

11

ABRAHAM
JOSHUA HESCHEL

Prophetic Mysticism

All events are secretly interrelated;
the sweep of all we are doing
reaches beyond the horizon of our comprehension.

–ABRAHAM JOSHUA HESCHEL[98]

Can mystics be prophets too?[99] Can hearing the inner voice of God inspire prophetic utterances intended to awaken people to the Divine will for their lives and their nation? Is spirituality as much about prophetic restlessness as contemplative calm?

The United States was born in protest. While our founding parents' protests were mixed with self-interest and racism as well as altruism and sacrifice, the founding of our nation was grounded in challenging the status quo in order to achieve a more perfect union in which all people could experience "life, liberty, and the pursuit of happiness." Today, the United States still aspires to greatness, and that aspiration inspires restlessness and impatience with the status quo.

People who fight for environmental justice and a future for future generations proclaim that they cannot let the slow political machinations determine the pace of change. Right now, in the words of June Jordan's poem honoring the protests against apartheid by South African women, "we are the ones that we have been waiting for." We must be contemplative activists for the well-being of our nation and the planet.

If God is still speaking, then there will always be a need for prophets, spiritual leaders who call our nation to its highest ideals and challenge anything that stands in the way of human dignity and planetary survival. Prayer and protest, contemplation and challenge, are the yin and yang of the American spiritual journey.

> *Our goal should be to live life in radical amazement . . . get up in the morning and look at the world in a way that takes nothing for granted. Everything is phenomenal; everything is incredible. . . . To be spiritual is to be amazed.*
>
> —ABRAHAM JOSHUA HESCHEL[100]

The Life of Abraham Heschel

Abraham Joshua Heschel (1907 –1972) believed he was called to embody for our time the voice of the Hebraic prophets. He experienced God's pain at the suffering of God's children, whether in Selma, Alabama, or South Vietnam. God's word could not be confined to the synagogue or sanctuary but must resound across the neighborhood and the nation, addressing individual people in terms of their specific personal and political challenges. He felt himself called to become a contemplative activist, speaking God's challenging words to a wayward nation.

Born to a respected lineage of rabbinical teachers going back to the founding of Hasidic Judaism, Heschel sought to integrate the joyful spirituality of the Baal Shem Tov,[101] for whom all things revealed God's light, with the recognition of human sin and limitation described by Moses Mendelssohn.[102] The wonder we perceive at the depth of spiritual experience exists in dynamic balance with the injustice and pain we observe (and from which we often benefit).

Raised in Poland before he immigrated to the United States, Heschel's early life was not easy. Despite his family being members of the spiritual elite, the untimely death of his father plunged the family into near poverty. Thanks to the generosity of a relative, Heschel continued his rabbinical studies and eventually received his doctorate, just as restrictions were being placed on Jewish academics.

Heschel saw himself as "a brand plucked from the fire of the altar to Satan on which my people was burned to death."[103] By providence, chance, and initiative, he avoided the flames of the Holocaust. He sought asylum in the United States and became part of a group of eight refugees given academic appointments at the Hebrew Union College in Cincinnati, Ohio. Meanwhile, tragically, Heschel's mother and surviving sister died in the Holocaust.

His daughter Susannah wrote, "I am still amazed by my father's courage, after losing his family in the war, to fall in love, marry and have a child." She went on to say:

I must add: he was never depressed, never moody or withdrawn or melancholy. Our family home was filled with laughter, jokes and playfulness. . . . Despair is forbidden, he used to say. God is everywhere and never gives us a task without also giving us the strength to carry it out.[104]

Destined for the rabbinate because of his spiritual pedigree, Heschel eventually transcended his orthodox roots to become an "apostle to the Gentiles," sharing the message of the Jewish prophets and mystics in interfaith contexts. Described as a spiritual radical, Heschel knew firsthand the evils of injustice, racism, and state-sponsored terrorism. He also knew that he must challenge political policies that deface the holiness of God's beloved children.

In the unfolding of his professional career, Heschel joined piety with a concern for social transformation. The walls of the sanctuary cannot contain God, Heschel believed; God must be worshipped through acts of hospitality and compassion in both personal relationships and political involvement. Heschel challenged the persecution of Jews in the Soviet Union, the United States' neglect of Jewish refugees from Germany, the nuclear arms race, Jim Crow laws and racial injustice, and the Vietnam War. For the contemplative intellectual, prayer leads to protest, and study leads to social concern.

When someone asked Heschel why he was demonstrating against the war in Vietnam, he replied, "I am here because I cannot pray." When asked to explain what he meant, he said, "Whenever I open the prayer book, I see images of children burning from napalm."[105]

On another occasion, Heschel asked his seminar students: "Gentlemen, what is your opinion, is gelatin kosher or not?" After a lively confabulation among the rabbinical students on Jewish dietary restrictions, Heschel then asked, "Is an atomic bomb kosher or not?"[106] When the students were unable to give him an answer, he concluded: "To speak about God and to remain silent on [war] is blasphemous." He believed true spirituality requires awakening to the Living God, who constantly pursues us, posing questions such as, "What will we do with our lives? How will we respond to the suffering we observe?"

Divinity, Heschel believed, is profoundly historical. God is concerned with the details of our personal lives and the machinations of politics as they shape the social order. In the spirit of the prophets, God cares about health-care reform, immigration and refugee assistance, the growing gap between rich and poor, the quality of education, social incivility, disinformation and demagoguery, white supremacy, science denial, and life in the inner city.

In contrast to the changeless perfection of Aristotle's unfeeling and unsympathetic Unmoved Mover, Heschel saw God as the Most-Moved Mover, who rejoices in our celebrations and grieves with our losses. Accordingly, Heschel, like Howard Thurman, believed that spiritual experiences plunge us into the tumult and messiness of politics, economics, and foreign policy. The God who constantly interacts with humankind in the events of history calls us to be spiritually minded social transformers.

Mysticism, our quest to experience the Living God, is embodied in political action and justice-seeking. Heschel described his experience marching with Martin Luther King Jr. in Selma, Alabama, with the words, "I felt like my legs were praying." Heschel captured the heart of American spirituality with its recognition of the significance of history as the realm of Divine activity.

Moreover, Heschel affirmed the role of humanity as God's companions in healing the world. Although utterly dependent on Divine creativity and compassion for our existence and well-being, our actions are also essential to the realization of God's vision for the world. We are God's hands and feet. We are God's advocates for justice and prophets of protest. When we save a soul by relieving the suffering of someone who's experiencing injustice, racism, poverty, and marginalization, we save the world. Conversely, when our political policies promote injustice, exclusion, violence, and racism, we participate in the world's destruction and the exile of God from history. When one soul is destroyed, God's impact on the world is diminished.

Radical Amazement

Plato asserted that philosophy begins with wonder; Heschel would add that theology also begins with wonder. When we, with the author of Psalm 8, gaze at the heavens and wonder whether we matter in the grand scheme of things, we are filled with amazement. When we pause to reflect on the complexity of human life, we proclaim with the author of Psalm 139:14, that humans in general and my own existence is "fearfully and wonderfully made." At such moments, we can't help but join Louis Armstrong in affirming that we live in a wonderful world.

At the heart of Heschel's mystical vision is the experience of radical amazement, the recognition that life itself is miraculous and that the foundations of all life depend on a wise Providence moving through all Creation. In describing the values that motivated his spiritual quest, Heschel noted, "I did not ask for success, I asked for wonder. And you gave it to me."[108] Wonder is essential to both spirituality and theology: "Awe is a sense of transcendence, for the reverence everywhere to mystery beyond all things. It enables us to perceive in the world intimations of the Divine."[109] God's wise creativity bursts forth everywhere and in all things. As Isaiah discovered in his mystical encounter with God, in every nook and cranny, noticed or unnoticed, angels sing:

> Holy, holy, holy is [Yahweh, God of cooperation and order[110]]; the whole earth is full of his glory. (6:3)

The wonder of all being, including my own being, leads to radical amazement at God's handiwork. Divinity is not aloof but present in every person as the deepest reality. Divine wisdom and providence come to us in all things. Even in God's apparent absence, Divinity serves as the crucible, making space for human creativity. Created in the image of God, we are ourselves amazing. As Heschel noted: "Just to be is a blessing. Just to live is holy. The moment is a marvel."[111]

Wonder leads to spirituality and ethics. Injustice and oppression reflect a deficiency of wonder. The perspective that life is a win-lose transaction, something to be manipulated, wreaks havoc on nations and families. Unable to acknowledge the ubiquitous wonder of all being, our society seeks to control and manipulate the world. Ultimately, our disenchantment leads to death and destruction.

According to Hasidic wisdom, a rabbi was once asked, "Where is God?" To which he answered, "Wherever we let him in." The practice of prayer "takes us out of normal self-interest and enables us to see the world in the mirror of the holy . . . we can behold a situation from the aspect of God."[112] Imperfect as we are, prayer awakens us to the holiness of others. It opens us to God's presence in the world and reveals to us our interdependence with all Creation. We learn to see the "thou" in what would otherwise be an "it" (to use the language of Heschel's friend and fellow mystic Martin Buber). We treasure the uniqueness of other people, cultures, and religions as reflective of Divine providence.

Experiences of radical amazement take us beyond ourselves and our tendency to see the world in terms of our own needs and desires. In seeing things from a God's-eye view, we experience the Divine pain at the suffering and injustice of the world. "Wonder leads to piety, and piety to holy deeds."[113] The Holy One who gives life to all things is a lively, passionate Becoming, intimately involved in the affairs of humans and nations. Divine creativity counteracts anything that stands in the way of human wholeness. When we ask for wonder, we commit ourselves to embodying our vocation as God's partners in healing the world.

The Passionate God

Western Christian theology is a marriage of two very different partners—the Greek philosophical vision and Judaism's lively historical activism. The Platonic tradition described timeless, static forms as the focus of the spiritual life, rather than the animated processes of a God who lives and moves in all things. Aristotle said the Divine is an unmoved mover, and any Divine interaction with the world would sully God's perfection. Throughout Western history, Christianity has struggled, with varying degrees of success, to join its Jewish and Greek roots.

Dear Lord, grant me the grace of wonder. Surprise me, amaze me, awe me in every crevice of your universe. Each day enrapture me with your marvelous things without number. . . . I do not ask to see the reason for it all. I ask only to share the wonder of it all.

—ABRAHAM JOSHUA HESCHEL[114]

Philosophers and theologians have noted that our images of God shape our spiritual and ethical focus. We become like the gods we imagine and behave like the gods we worship. Thanks to the Greek influence, Western Christianity has given us a God who is unchanging, omnipotent, and omniscient, while often neglecting the relational aspects of God. Focusing on a transcendent, all-powerful God tends to maintain the social status quo. Meanwhile, people who conceive of God as pure, unchanging Being often see the mystical path as a journey from the alone to the Alone. From this perspective, spiritual maturity draws us away from the helter-skelter of politics, economics, and domestic life to the stillness of the spiritual hermitage or monastery. Authoritarian images of God promote authoritarian styles of political and ecclesiastical leadership.

Morally speaking, there is no limit to the concern one must feel for the suffering of human beings, that indifference to evil is worse than evil itself, that in a free society, some are guilty, but all are responsible.

—ABRAHAM JOSHUA HESCHEL[115]

Relational images of God, on the other hand, inspire democratic behaviors and concern for our fellow creatures. The God of the prophets and Jesus is lively and historical, constantly interacting with the world, shaping and adapting to the concreteness of life. This active and involved Divinity encourages creativity, change, and protest. Perfection is found in compassion rather than isolation, intimacy rather than independence.

Abraham Joshua Heschel, like Howard Thurman and John Woolman, saw God as the most moved mover. Fidelity to God involves immersing ourselves in the world of change and politics. While attending to the unchanging and eternal, most especially God's faithfulness and care for Creation, is an aspect of the spiritual journey, the role of the eternal is also to give us a broad perspective and moral compass for our spiritual involvement in an ever-changing world. Wonder and piety, as Heschel noted, are completed in good works, performed in the uncertain and constantly shifting onslaught of historical events.

For Heschel, who learned from the Hebraic prophets, spirituality is inherently relational and passionate—because God is relational and passionate. Prayer, he said, is the quest to experience God, to feel God's feelings, and to respond to God's questions, all of which are timebound and concrete.

Heschel had this to say about Divine questions:

When faith is completely replaced by creed, worship by discipline, love by habit; when the crisis of today is ignored because of the splendor of the past; when faith becomes an heirloom rather than a living fountain; when religion speaks only in the name of authority rather than with the voice of compassion—its message becomes meaningless. Religion is an answer to humanity's ultimate questions. [We need] to rediscover the questions to which religion is an answer.

Human life is constantly confronted by these questions. Ethics and spirituality involve how we respond to the questions and possibilities God places before us in every moment of our lives. Profoundly embedded in the world, and deeply touched by our joy and pain, God has "skin in the game." Divinity is passionate about bringing wholeness and justice to both inner lives and outer behaviors.

Twenty-five hundred years before Heschel, the author of Lamentations highlighted the paradox of Divine changelessness combined with Divine newness.

The steadfast love of [Yahweh] never ceases, his mercies never come to an end; they are new every morning; great is your faithfulness. (3:22–23)

God's love is eternal—and at the same time, God's presence is historical, contextual, and dynamic. The Infinite is the Intimate; the Most Eternal is also the Most Relative.

Prayer is meaningles unless it is subversive, unless it seeks to overthrow and to ruin the pyramids of callousness, hatred, opportunism, falsehoods . . . the forces that continue to destroy the promise, the hope, the vision.

—ABRAHAM JOSHUA HESCHEL[116]

Heschel coined the term *Divine Pathos* to describe God's relationship with the world. He wrote:

Pathos denotes not an idea of goodness, but of loving care; not an immutable example, but an ongoing challenge, a dynamic relation between God and [humanity] . . . a passionate summons.[117]

The Divine Pathos is God's radical empathy with the world.

God's joy and sorrow emerge in relationship to human activities. God hears the cries of the poor and suffers along with the neglected and maligned. God feels the pain of homeless families, farmers whose farms have been foreclosed, and single parents who live from paycheck to paycheck. Divinity experiences the grief of families when loved ones die of COVID-19 and the terror of children in war-torn nations. The Giver of All Life knows the death of dreams among inner-city children and Appalachian teenagers, and bombs in Syria and Afghanistan shake the Holy One to the core. God weeps for the plight of refugees who are refused entrance into the United States and children who are separated from their parents at our borders. Divinity was beaten on the Edmund Pettis Bridge and incinerated at Auschwitz.

> *God is not a concept produced by deliberation. God is an outcry wrung from heart and mind; God is never an explanation; it is always a challenge. It can only be uttered in astonishment. . . . The word "God" is an assault, a thunder in the soul, not a notion to play with.*
>
> —ABRAHAM JOSHUA HESCHEL[118]

God challenges the apathy of the rich and reminds them that their failure to hear the cries of the poor will lead to a famine of hearing the word of God. According to the prophet Amos, the spiritual cost of apathy and injustice will eventually come due:

The time is surely coming, says [Yahweh], when I will send a famine on the land; not a famine of bread, or a thirst for water, but of hearing the words of [Yahweh]. They shall wander from sea to sea, and from north to east; they shall run to and fro, seeking the word of [Yahweh], but they shall not find it. (8:11–12)

Given America's history of genocide, slavery, Jim Crow, redlining, economic injustice, and political demagoguery, Heschel believed the nation needed to take to heart these verses from Amos. The current national incivility and divisiveness, not to mention the rise of white Christian nationalism and the undermining of democratic struc- tures by self-interested politicians, is an indictment of our nation's waywardness. Many congregations claiming the name "Christian" portray blatant social and environmental evils as God's will. Repentance and turning from self-inter- est to world loyalty is our only hope. It is also God's hope. God needs us, according to Heschel, to bring justice and well-being to the world. God needs us to be companions in mending the world.

When we are inattentive to the Divine vision of heal- ing and abundance, when we purposely turn our backs on justice, we limit what God can do in the world. We exile God to the sidelines, marginalizing the impact of Divinity on our lives. Meanwhile, God wants to be on the frontlines, guiding us in the paths of justice and restoration.

God is in all things—but at the same time, all things are present in God, shaping the Divine experience for good or for ill. God is alive and relational, involved and concerned about what happens here on earth, and seeking justice in the everyday details of economics and relationships. God, Heschel wrote, does not self-reveal "in abstract aloofness, but in personal and intimate relationship with the world." God "does not simply command and expect obedience," but "is also moved and affected by what happens in the world, and reacts accordingly."[119]

Prophetic Spirituality

While there are many models of mysticism and spirituality, Heschel's unique contribution is his focus on prophetic spirituality. Prophets are people who are given insights into God's vision for the world. The Living God feels the world's pain, and people who follow God are especially empathetic toward those who experience injustice, illness, discrimination, or neglect. Prophetic impatience reflects the Divine passion for justice.

"Prophecy," said Heschel, "is the voice God has lent to the silent agony, a voice to the plundered poor." He went on to say:

Faith is not the clinging to a shrine but an endless pilgrimage of the heart. Audacious longing, burning songs, daring thoughts, an impulse overwhelming the heart usurping the mind—these are all a drive towards serving the One who rings our hearts like a bell.

—ABRAHAM JOSHUA HESCHEL[120]

In speaking, the prophet reveals God. This is the marvel of a prophet's work: in [their] words, the invisible God becomes audible. Divine power bursts in [their] words. The authority of the prophet is in the Presence [their] words reveal.[121]

Contemplation is not enough. Prayer must hit the streets. Our spirituality must take shape in protests, marches, sacrificial living, and advocacy. There is no ultimate distinction between spirituality and politics and the individual and the communal in prophetic faith. Encountering God is not an escape from the messiness of politics and economics, but a challenge to heal institutions as well as people. Accordingly, Heschel's spirituality compelled him to march in Selma, challenge the nuclear arms race, and publicly oppose the Vietnam War.

"The prophet's word is a scream in the night," Heschel wrote.

> While the world is at ease and asleep, the prophet feels the blast from heaven. The prophet faces a coalition of callousness and established authority and undertakes to stop a mighty stream with mere words. The purpose of prophecy is to conquer callousness, to change the inner person as well as to revolutionize history.[122]

In the interplay of God's call and human response, the prophet experiences the world from God's perspective, looking beyond self-interest, comfort, and nationalism to embody God's will in the affairs of people and nations. The personal God is always calling to us, and when we turn to God's way, God's vision becomes the primary lens through which we experience the world. The prophet is both a messenger and witness, and the prophetic witness is grounded in the experience of God's call to heal the Earth and its people. "The prophet," Heschel wrote, "is a person who suffers the harm done to others. Wherever a crime is committed, it is as if the prophet were the victim and the prey. All prophecy is one great exclamation: God is not indifferent to evil!"[123]

Prophetic spirituality shares in God's sympathy and pathos. For the prophet, each moment is decisive because each moment touches the heart of God. Political and economic structures are especially important to the prophets because of their impact on the planet and its creatures. A decision made in the White House can lead to the deaths of thousands of people, accelerate global climate change, and push the planet closer to nuclear annihilation. It can also ensure that children have sufficient food, families have secure homes, and adequate medical care is available to all.

The Bible's prophets remind us that spirituality opens us to the world's pain. Jesus wept over the death of his dear friend Lazarus and the hardheartedness of Jerusalem's religious and political leaders. Amos, Hosea, and Micah felt the pain of the forgotten and marginalized, the tears of homeless farmers and starving widows. Always, the prophet's harshest words are aimed at religious leaders and institutions that connect God's blessing with economic prosperity, while turning away people in need.

Spiritual experiences deepen our faith and our sense of God's presence in our lives; they also open our hearts to the pain of the world

> *The road to the sacred leads through the secular.*
>
> —ABRAHAM JOSHUA HESCHEL[125]

and the disparity between God's visions and our nation's actions.

Few of us choose to be prophets. It is painful and dangerous work. Yet all of us, Heschel believed, are challenged to be prophetic in taking responsibility for our nation's actions and the institutions of which we are a part. As Heschel proclaimed: "Let there be a grain of prophet in everyone!"[124]

The meaning of the Sabbath is to celebrate time rather than space. Six days a week we live under the tyranny of things of space; on the Sabbath we try to become attuned to holiness in time. It is a day on which we are called upon to share in what is eternal in time, to turn from the results of creation to the mystery of creation; from the world of creation to the creation of the world.

—ABRAHAM JOSHUA HESCHEL[128]

Celebrating Sabbath

God is a timely God who inspires both action and rest. History as the theatre of Divine activity is intended to be sanctified. Heschel described Judaism as a "religion of time aiming at the sanctification of time."[126]

To balance their commitment to social transformation, prophets must take time for rest. Following God's way involves immersing ourselves in human need; it also requires time for quiet prayer, family life, and study. The Bible refers to this time as *Sabbath*, a time when work ceases, when we restore our minds, bodies, and spirits.

On the Sabbath, we become attuned to holiness in history, our own and our planet's. We dedicate ourselves to letting go, so that we learn to praise and to listen to the deeper voice of God within us. Sabbath is a holy day, a day of grace that inspires us to personal and planetary transformation. In stillness, we hear God's voice. In play and relaxation, we experience the deeper identities of our children, partners, and friends. We return to the Source from which energy and insight flow. A contemplative day, the Sabbath orients and reorients. It turns us from self-interest to God's vision, and it gives us direction for the next steps of our journey. Heschel referred to the Sabbath as "a realm of time where the goal is not to have but to be, not to own but to give, not to control but to share, not to subdue but to be in accord."[127]

Sabbath keeping inspires concern for the welfare of other people who make our own lives possible. During the COVID pandemic, I gained a new appreciation for "essential workers," many of whom, such as farmworkers, warehouse workers, and nursing home caregivers, were undocumented residents. I recognized that many of these workers received minimum wages, worked long hours, and risked their lives to maintain the food distribution chain. Prophetic sabbath keeping inspired religious leaders to champion workers' rights, safe working conditions, health insurance and social security, child labor laws, vacations, and shorter work weeks.

The Path of Prophetic Mysticism

The realization of the American dream depends on the ongoing critique from those who join prayer and protest, contemplation and challenge so that all might enjoy "life, liberty, and the pursuit of happiness."

Abraham Joshua Heschel embodied the spirit of the Hebraic prophets who heard God's voice, listened, and then spoke. They experienced the contrast between God's dream of Shalom and the waywardness of people and nations. The events of history reflect the tension of God's call and human response. God is alive, concerned, and challenges us to live up to God's image within ourselves and those around us. God feels the joy and pain of the Earth and its creatures, and in encountering God, we feel God's pain and joy and are inspired to be God's companions in *tikkun olam*, mending the world. God confronts us with questions, "What will you do to respond to the cries of the poor? Will you stand with the stranger and immigrant, the marginalized and bullied? How will you speak for the voiceless in the human and nonhuman world?"

Prayer is not a stratagem for occasional use, a refuge to resort to now and then. It is rather like an established residence for the innermost self. All things have a home: the bird has a nest, the fox has a hole, the bee has a hive. A soul without prayer is a soul without a home.

—ABRAHAM JOSHUA HESCHEL[129]

It has been said that the distinction between ignorance and apathy can be found in the phrases, "I don't know" and "I don't care." Today, it is difficult to be ignorant of the pain of the world and the willful injustice and incivility in our land. A few minutes ago, I heard another report on the impact of intentional COVID-19 disinformation in the spike of cases in the United States. I mourned the death of a Capitol police officer by suicide in the wake of the January 6 insurrection, and the current attempts to deny the involvement of political leaders in inciting these treasonous behaviors. I viewed forest fires in the West, in part, the result of global climate change and the failure of our leaders to prevent a crisis that will forever change our children's and grandchildren's lives.

God is asking, along with the generations to come, "Where are you in tipping the balance from hate to love and from destruction to healing?"

While few of us may claim the title "prophet," the survival of the American democracy and the planet depends on our taking up the prophetic mantle in ways appropriate to our life situation, abilities, and personality. Today, as loyal Americans and planetary citizens, we can embody Heschel's prophetic spirituality by:

- prayerfully listening to the news on television or the radio and not turning away from troubling issues.

- seeing the Divine image in those who suffer from institutional injustice and neglect.

- looking deeper into the news, often from a variety of sources, to experience our kinship with those described.

- taking time to go beyond the headlines to explore the real issues at stake in issues of injustice, demagoguery, racism, and environmental destruction (for Heschel and the Jewish tradition, study is a necessity in political involvement and can be a form of prayer).

- asking for God's guidance in responding to the pain we see in the media.

- responding with acts of kindness and social concern and, if appropriate, advocacy, protest, and civil disobedience.

Prayer of Awareness and Transformation

God of all Creation, human and nonhuman,
wake me up to the pain of the world.
Jar me from complacency and complicity.
Help me see the pain of the world as your pain
and challenge me to respond with courage and grace,
to alleviate the pain of the world
and be your companion in healing the Earth.

12

MADELEINE L'ENGLE

Spirituality on a Swiftly Tilting Planet

*We do not draw people to Christ
by loudly discrediting what they believe,
by telling them how wrong they are and how right we are,
but by showing them a light that is so lovely
that they want with all their hearts
to know the source of it.*

—MADELEINE L'ENGLE[130]

Madeleine L'Engle asserted that "the sense of wonder is a prayer."[131] When we look at the heavens above, photos from the Hubble Telescope, or peer into our own immune systems through an electron microscope, amazement fills our minds. Whether we consider the 13.7-billion-year, trillion-galaxy universe story, or the reality that the wholeness of our ever-expanding universe got its start in a flash of energy no longer than our fingernail, we are overwhelmed with wonder. Our soul sings out when we discover that the universe-within—our cells, immune system, and firing neurons—and the universe-beyond defy our wildest imaginations.

While many people feel "lost in the cosmos," to quote author Walker Pearcy, mystics experience the universe as chockful of Divinity. Although mystics recognize their fallibility and mortality, they also realize the whole Earth is full of God's glory. The Bible portrays the mystic vision from the first words of Genesis, when God spoke forth the universe and declared it good, to the final words of Revelation, in which the exiled John of Patmos was confronted by the Alpha and Omega and realized that despite persecution and violence, God would wipe every tear from our eyes. The prologue of John's Gospel proclaims a God-filled universe:

> In the beginning was the Word, and the Word was with God, and the Word was God. He was in the beginning with God. All things came into being through him, and without him not one thing came into being. What has come into being in him was life, and the life was the light of all people. The light shines in the darkness, and the darkness did not overcome it. . . . The true light, which enlightens everyone, was coming into the world. And the Word became flesh and lived among us, and we have seen his glory, the glory as of a father's only son, full of grace and truth. (1:1-5, 9, 14)

In my Christmas meditations in 2017, I took a month to explore the mysticism of Madeleine L'Engle. As I read her words each morning between December 25 and January 6, I was inspired by her affirmation of the Incarnation. God takes flesh in a humble stable, enabling all Creation to become the icon of Divinity.[132] Pondering the wonder of the Word and Wisdom of God incarnate in our world, she rejoiced, "The neutrino comes to heal and bless. The neutrino danced the night Christ was born."[133] Divine light permeates, enlivens, and enlightens all things. Quoting Saint Bonaventure, one of the many mystics to make this affirmation, L'Engle affirmed with other mystis: "God is a circle whose center is everywhere and whose circumference is nowhere."[134] For L'Engle (and the other mystics described in this book), the universe finds its center

God is constantly calling us to be more than we are.

—MADELEINE L'ENGLE[135]

in God, whose energy and wisdom give life to all things and whose love embraces every creature. God's light shines in the darkness, making even the darkest situation a place of growth and transformation. Love inspires the scientist, theologian, mystic, and artist. It also inspires children as they imagine themselves to be a soccer star or a unicorn.

Mystics are not passive but experience their divinity in moments of creativity in which they discover themselves to be co-creators with the Artist of the Universe. When we bring beauty to the world through art, music, or writing, we contribute to God's goal of healing the universe, one day and planet at a time.

The Life of Madeleine L'Engle

Madeleine L'Engle Camp (1918–2007) was born to a family of both privilege and challenge. Her parents could afford to send her, sometimes to her sorrow and chagrin, to boarding schools and provide her with a strong literary and intellectual foundation. Her father was a journalist, foreign correspondent, detective story writer, and literary critic, with many social and cultural connections among the elite of his time. Yet, he was also plagued with poor health, due to contact with mustard gas while serving in Europe during World War I. Madeleine's father died when she was seventeen and away from home in boarding school.

I need a God who is with us always, everywhere, in the deepest depths as well as the highest heights. It is when things go wrong, when good things do not happen, when our prayers seem to have been lost, that God is most present. We do not need the sheltering wings when things go smoothly. We are closest to God in the darkness, stumbling along blindly.

—MADELEINE L'ENGLE[136]

L'Engle confesses that although she was steeped in Anglican liturgy, she had little formal religious training as a child. In many ways, she believed that the lack of childhood catechetical instruction was a gift. She had little to unlearn later in life and could come to faith with fresh eyes, without the confines of biblical literalism or narrow-minded prejudice.

As a young person, Madeleine L'Engle was a bit like a geode: her inner beauty was often hidden by her nondescript exterior. Like Charles Wallace, the young adventurer of her Time Trilogy texts, she was often underestimated by her teachers, who seldom saw her as a budding intellectual or promising writer. She was criticized for "coloring outside the lines" when her responses to assignments were too imaginative or creative to fit into the academic boxes constructed by her teachers.

Throughout her life, imagination was the pathway to personal growth and spiritual formation. As an adult, she recognized that our visions of God are often too small. We live in a wondrous, mysterious, and wild universe that constantly presents us with personal and cosmic "impossibilities." We need to let our hearts and minds "grow in wisdom and stature," as did Jesus, to encompass God's revelation in the breadth of emerging galaxies and the firing of neurons in our brains. The fruits of spirituality are not only love and justice but also imagination and creativity.

While studying at Smith College, Madeleine began to find her voice and discover her vocation. After her graduation from college, she sought a career in the New York theatre, while also nurturing her gifts as a writer. During her theatre years, she met and married a fellow actor, Hugh Franklin (1916–1986), best known for his role as Dr. Charles Tyler in the long-running soap opera *All My Children*.

In the early 1950s, Madeleine and Hugh left Manhattan to live in Goshen, Connecticut, where they ran a general store, and Madeleine served as the choir director of the local Congregational church. Although she published a handful of books by her mid-thirties, she almost gave up writing at forty, believing she needed to carry her weight in the family finances. Finally, literary success came with the award-winning A *Wrinkle in Time*, published (after twenty-six rejections) in 1962.

Like Whitman, Emerson, Dickinson, and Thoreau, Madeleine L'Engle's mysticism inspired and guided her vocation as a writer. Though best known for her young adult books, L'Engle also sought to convey the wisdom of scripture, spirituality, and science to adult readers. A creative synthesis of cosmology, literature, and spiritual reflection informed her writing and spiritual journey. As a young child, her father woke her up in the middle of the night to show her a night full of stars—and for the rest of her life, the wonder of Creation, both intergalactic and cellular, inspired her. The heavens declare the glory of God—and so do the cells of our bodies.

L'Engle eventually wrote more than thirty books, ranging from children's and young adult literature to poetry and spiritual reflections. Nothing was off-limits to her creative mind, whether in science, society, theology, or scripture.

L'Engle's spirituality was lived out in the daily tasks of marriage, parenting, and writing. Cognizant of her limitations, her constant spiritual companion was the Jesus Prayer: "Lord, have mercy upon me, a sinner." In the immensity of the universe, our lives are barely noticeable, yet the light of Divine creation—the Big Bang and the universe journey—flows intimately through the days of our lives.

After a serious auto accident in her seventies, L'Engle chanted the Jesus Prayer on her way to the hospital. She recalled:

I knew that once I went under the anesthetic I might not come out of it, not in this life. I was not afraid. The Jesus prayer was still with me, a strong rope to which I held like a sailor fallen from a ship. If God was ready for the curtain to come down on the final act of this life's drama, I was as ready as I was ever going to be. I am grateful for that feeling of readiness, for the assurance that whatever happened all would be well.[137]

Throughout her adult life, L'Engle's days began and ended with morning and evening prayers from the *Book of Common Prayer*. She described her evening prayer, the Office of Compline, as her "Go-to-Bed-Quietly-and-Fearlessly office."[138]

Her spirituality inspired her to revive an ancient spiritual practice, "kything," a reflection of the interdependence of the universe and the ties that bind us with every creature. In the practice of kything, an individual intimately joins another person, whether in the same room or across the universe.

L'Engle saw herself as a companion in God's quest to heal the Earth, reflected in her commitment to silent listening for Divine inspiration and her regular practice of visualizing people and situations in terms of wholeness and possibility. Often her Earth prayers involved seeing the planet through the Divine eye, healed as God intended it to be.

L'Engle's vocation as a writer was a form of co-creativity with the Divine. God paints on the large canvas of the universe—and we bring beauty, order, and healing to our own little worlds. Divine creativity, bringing order out of chaos as the pathway to beauty, is our model for spiritual artistry, whether lived out in writing, teaching, working for world peace, or bringing joy to our families.

God Is Present Everywhere

Emmanuel means "God is with us"—but it also means that God is in us, around us, and moving through us. God's presence in the world is intimate, nonlinear, and nonlocal. Madeleine L'Engle experienced all things in God and God in all things. She summarized her vision of God through the words of eleventh-century theologian Hildevert of Lavardin:

> *God is over all things,*
> *under all things,*
> *outside all,*
> *within, but not enclosed,*
> *without, but not excluded,*
> *above, but not raised up,*
> *below, but not depressed,*
> *wholly above, presiding,*
> *wholly without, embracing,*
> *wholly within, filling.*[139]

L'Engle was an incarnational mystic. She believed the Word made flesh in Jesus of Nazareth best describes God's relationship to the world and God's invitation for us to experience and express our inner divinity and Divine destination. According to L'Engle:

> I believe we can understand cosmic questions only through particulars. I can understand only through one particular, the incarnation of Jesus of Nazareth. This is the ultimate particular, which gives me my understanding of the Creator and the beauty of life. I believe that God loved us so much that he came to us as a human being, as one of us, to show us his love.[140]

In the spirit of the early church, L'Engle believed God became human so humans might become divine; with his life, Jesus blessed and sanctified every season of human experience. Incarnational spirituality makes the secular sacred and invites us to be like Christ. "The Maker of the universe or perhaps many universes," she wrote, "willingly and lovingly" left power and privilege behind and came "to show us what we ought to be and could be."[141]

As a young person, L'Engle experienced Christ as a palpable companion, whose presence assured her all would be well, despite the challenges of her father's illness and her inability to fit in with her peers or teachers. She wrote in her book on incarnation:

> One day, I was in the bedroom, standing at the basin, washing my hands. And Jesus was there. In the bathroom with me. Telling me without words that it was alright and that there was work for me to do. I did not

question his presence. . . . Why didn't he come to me in church? Or when I was saying my prayers? Or even in the park? Somewhere more appropriate.[142]

L'Engle discovered that the Incarnate One was the truly Loving One, even in the bathroom!

A true experience of God connects us with each other, healing the schisms in the fabric of human existence. L'Engle's belief in this reality caused her to affirm: "Wherever there is love, there is Jesus.," which then triggered her to ask: "Are there planets where people have grown up loving God and Creation and each other? Where religion binds people together instead of tearing them apart?"[143]

The Loving God is embodied in every creature—from the amoeba to the elephant, from the newborn baby to the bloviating politician. Deep down, we are all mystics, intimately connected to God, but many of us have ignored that aspect of ourselves for so long that we can hardly believe it exists. Most of the time, we are unaware that the Heart of God beats within our hearts or that the Mind of Christ is our deepest reality.

Nothing, no one, is too small to matter. What you do is going to make a difference.

—MADELEINE L'ENGLE[146]

The nature of the Incarnation will always be a mystery, and yet, as L'Engle wrote: "We do not have to understand anything except that the Maker loves us enough to become part of us."[144] God truly cares for "every atom and subatom of creation."[145] The Mystery of God is made of love.

God's intimate relationship with all things joins mysticism and ethics. If God is present as the deepest reality of all things, then we can experience the holiness of every aspect of Creation, even those people, places, or circumstances that seem most alien to us. Even the most difficult person exists moment by moment as a manifestation of God's love, inspiring us to affirmation and care, despite the appearance of insignificance or ugliness.

L'Engle often prayed as she walked from her Manhattan apartment to the library at the Cathedral of St. John the Divine. One prayer she regularly invoked acknowledges the mystery of God's Word becoming flesh. She confessed: "I look at whomever is nearest to me so that I may see in that person, for that moment, Christ."

Nothing loved is ever lost or perished.

—MADELEINE L'ENGLE[148]

One morning, as L'Engle and her dog walked to the Cathedral, a tattered man, frightened by her gentle dog, began hitting the dog. After ensuring the safety of her dog, she nervously blessed the man, and he ran off.

A passerby asked, "Is he mad?"

"Out of his mind," the shaken L'Engle replied. Then, in a moment of inspiration, she realized: "No matter how crazed he was, that man had to be Christ for me. If I cannot see Christ in the maimed, in those possessed by devils, I cannot see Christ in the whole and holy."[147] The Incarnation inspires a mysticism of presence in which Divine reality is present in everyone and everything, and God loves all things. All that exists matters, and God treasures it forever.

Gentle Interdependence

A sense of unity with the Holy is at the heart of mystical experiences. God is not far off but as near as your next breath and the next person you meet.

For L'Engle, unity with all Creation was central to her spiritual vision. All things—body, mind, spirit—are connected. We are joined with the plankton and mitochondria, and we are equally intertangled with galaxies and the dark energy of the universe. According to L'Engle, "We do not exist in isolation. We are part of a vast web of relationships and interrelationships which sing themselves in ancient harmonies."[149]

Contemporary cosmology and physics, central to L'Engle's understanding of God's unfolding creation, present the vision of a vast, intricate, interconnected process of evolution at both the micro and the macro levels of life. Spirituality awakens us to this universe, in which the Earth is filled with God's glory, and each thing we see is enchanted with the wonder of the Divine Mystery. Encountering God awakens us to our relationship with all Creation. In A *Ring of Endless Light*, L'Engle describes this spiritual vision, once considered to be archaic and superstitious, through Vicki Austin's kything—her empathetic communication—with two dolphins.

The mystics live in a world of praise, grounded in the gentle and sometimes wild interdependence of life. The mysticism of dolphins and humans alike reflects what scientists now describe as the butterfly effect, in which every personal change radiates across the universe; our spiritual lives can tip the balance from death to life at the cellular or cosmic levels of existence.

Mystics, poets, dolphins, scientists, and little children, all show us the way, L'Engle believed, to a spirituality of interdependence, in which each of us both uniquely matters and is at the same time one with everything else. God is the glue that holds the universe together, his energetic wisdom moving in all, through all, and beyond each and every creature. In mystic moments, our joining with the pulse of Creation inspires empathy and appreciation. We remember that within the body of Christ, there is no "other"; each individual's joys and sorrows send ripples through the entire universe. (The Latin word from which we get *universe—universus*—means "combined into one.")

Creating with God

In L'Engle's cosmic mysticism, every creature matters not only to its companions but to the cosmos itself. (The Latin root words of *cosmos* point to the universe being the embodiment of order and harmony.)

Scripture affirms that every creature matters to God, from the lilies of the field and the birds of the air to finite and fallible humans called by God to embrace impossible possibilities. Each one of us—tree or human—has a vocation to be God's companion and co-worker in the ongoing creation of beauty and love in the world. As L'Engle said:

> This is our calling, co-creation. Every single one of us, without exception, is called to co-create with God. No

one is too unimportant to have a share in the making or unmaking of the final shining-forth. Everything that we do either draws the Kingdom of love closer, or pushes it further off.[151]

L'Engle's vocation, her Divine calling, was writing.

Each of us also has a spiritual calling, a mystic vocation. We are called to use our unique gifts, whatever they may be, to contribute to the ongoing process of *tikkun olam*, the mending of the world.

Empathetic Imagination

Madeleine L'Engle's spirituality was grounded in the daily practice of silent listening for the Divine within herself and in others as she visualized God's healing of people and situations. She referred to this empathetic imagination as *kything*.

There is nothing so secular that it cannot be sacred, and that is one of the deepest messages of the Incarnation.

—MADELEINE L'ENGLE[152]

According to L'Engle, kything comes from an ancient Scottish word, describing a type of wordless communication, not limited by space or time. I wonder if kything reflects the Celtic notion of *anamchara*—friend of the soul—in which two souls, regardless of their distance from each other, feel a sense of spiritual unity. L'Engle described kything as "how cherubim talk. It's talking without words." Kything connects angels and other creatures with "you, with stars, with galaxies, with the salt in the ocean, the leaves in the trees."[153] Kything is the experiential revelation of the graceful interdependence of life, in which we are all joined by the One in whom we live and move and have our being, whose Spirit speaks to us in sighs too deep for words.

There are many ways to "kythe"—spiritually connect—with another person. For several years, for example, I shared a sense of unity with a spiritual friend who had been diagnosed with incurable cancer. Each morning as I walked on Craigville Beach, I affirmed and visualized her well-being as I gave her a short long-distance reiki healing-touch treatment. I felt a tangible bond, and she saw that our connection added to her health and longevity.

Naming is one of the impulses behind all art; to give a name to the cosmos we see despite all the chaos.

—MADELEINE L'ENGLE[154]

Whether you understand kything as intercessory prayer or telepathy, you might begin by simply asking God, "With whom do you wish me to connect spiritually?" You may already have someone in mind; if so, let them know you are praying for them or joining them empathetically. You might even let the person know your schedule for kything prayer so they can intentionally open themselves to your prayers and communicate wordlessly with you. My spiritual friend knew I would always prayerfully communicate with her between 6:00 a.m. and 7:00 a.m., while I was taking my sunrise beach walk.

In your practice, take a few minutes or more to visualize and name the person with whom you are connecting. Quietly feel the unity in Spirit you share, as you hold them in

God's healing and loving light. Feel the Spirit within you, joining you, to bring wholeness to both your lives. Conclude by holding the other person again in God's love. Experience God's peace flowing between you, and then commit their lives to God's care until you "meet again."

Prayer of Our Spiritual Home

Join me, Spirit of Life, with all Creation,
giving and receiving love
and discerning your presence in every encounter.
Let me feel the nearness of those I love
and bring only beauty into their lives.
Let me be a messenger of your wholeness and peace
to this good Earth.

13

MARY OLIVER

The Art of Seeing

It is a serious thing just to be alive.

—MARY OLIVER[155]

Throughout this text, I've mentioned more than once that vision plays a significant role in the mystical journey. The doors of perception are often clearer and wider during mystical experiences. The mystic experiences the Infinite that undergirds finite reality.

More than "all eye," mystical visions often involve sound, taste, touch, smell, and even the paranormal, as well as sight. "Taste and see" the goodness of God, the psalmist counsels. Touch can transform cells as well as souls, and the aroma of incense inspired the prophet Isaiah's encounter with the Holy One.

We live in a world of praise, proclaims Psalm 148:

Praise [Yahweh] from the earth,
you sea monsters and all deeps,
fire and hail, snow and frost,
stormy wind fulfilling his command!
Mountains and all hills, fruit trees and all cedars!
Wild animals and all cattle,
creeping things and flying birds! (verses 7–10)

Nonhumans as well as humans give glory to their Creator. "Let everything that breathes praise God! Praise God!" (Psalm 150:6).

Whether poet, social activist, naturalist, theologian, parent, or laborer, the mystic is an artist who sees holiness, infinity, and eternity in everyday, and time-bound experiences. While mysticism may involve times of withdrawal to purify the senses and attune our spirits to God, these times of contemplation inspire radical amazement. As Abraham Joshua Heschel asserted: Reality overflows with wonder, abundance, diversity, and challenge. When we learn to sense the Divine, we can, with nineteenth-century Jesuit poet Gerard Manley Hopkins, celebrate the "pied beauty of God," broadcast in every moment of life. We can, with Saint Francis of Assisi, experience God's creative love and artistry in all creatures and seasons of life, including death itself. And we may, like poet-mystic Mary Oliver, discover: "Glory is my work."[156]

Instructions for living a life:
Pay attention. Be astonished.
Tell about it

—MARY OLIVER[158]

The Life of Mary Oliver

Not bound by steeple and sanctuary or creed and ritual, Mary Oliver (1935–2019) believed the whole world is a manifestation of Divine creativity. Beyond and within the disenchanted world of human artifice and technology—the world of profit, power, and prestige—lies an enchanted reality, waiting to be discovered by those who have trained their senses to notice. As Oliver wrote, to truly live, we simply need to "Pay attention. Be astonished. Tell about it."[157] In this enchanted world, Oliver found her vocation as God's companion in beauty-making.

Born in Maple Hills, a suburb of Cleveland, Ohio, Mary Oliver was sensitive to the beauty and wonder of Nature from the time she was a child. She often retreated from what she described as a difficult childhood to the woods near her home, where she wrote poetry and built huts of sticks and grass. "When the high school I went to experienced a crisis of delinquent student behavior," Oliver recalled, "my response was to start out for school every morning but to turn most mornings into the woods instead, with a knapsack of books."[159]

Although school officials warned her parents that her truancy might delay her graduation, her parents let her go her own way. This allowed her to deepen her understanding of poetry while she drank deep from the solitary beauty of Nature. After high school, Oliver attended Ohio State University and Vassar College, but she did not graduate from either institution.

Edna St. Vincent Millay influenced her early poetry. This led to an opportunity to help the poet's sister Norma organize Millay's papers. She met her lifelong partner photographer Molly Malone Cook during this time, and the two settled in Provincetown, Massachusetts, where they lived until Cook's death in 2005.

> *To live in this world, you must be able to do three things: to love what is mortal; to hold it against your bones knowing your own life depends on it; and, when the time comes to let it go, to let it go.*
>
> —MARY OLIVER[160]

As a fellow Cape Codder, I appreciate Oliver's description of Provincetown: "I too fell in love with the town, that marvelous convergence of land and water; frighteningly small boats; and, both residents and sometime visitors, the many artists and writers."[161] The very private poet further noted:

> People say to me: wouldn't you like to see Yosemite? The Bay of Fundy? The Brooks Range? I smile and answer, "Oh yes—sometime," and go off to my woods, my ponds, my sun-filled harbor, no more than a blue comma on the map of the world but, to me, the emblem of everything.[162]

Throughout her life, Oliver garnered several prestigious poetry awards, including the Pulitzer Prize, the Guggenheim Foundation Fellowship, and the National Book Award for Poetry. She died in Florida of lymphoma at the age of eighty-three.

Graceful Interdependence and Universal Experience

Mary Oliver is the poetic apostle of interdependence and impermanence. She proclaimed that our planet is alive, and that nonhumans, including plants, not only experience their environments but can interact with a relational, embodied, and interdependent Deity.

Her worldview ran parallel with that of the psalmist's, who proclaimed that "the heavens declare the glory of God" (Psalm 19:1). "Sea monsters" (perhaps, the humpbacked whales sporting off Cape Cod shores!), "mountains and all hills, fruit trees and all cedars! Wild animals and all cattle, creeping things and flying birds!" also praise their Creator (Psalm 148:9–10).

Praise affirms the ability to experience Divinity in all Creation, great and small, and any form of experience. It undergirds value and significance, apart from human interests. Anything that can praise deserves ethical consideration, so say pan-experiential theologians like myself! (Pan-experientialism asserts that humans are not alone in an unfeeling universe but that the world is alive and filled with creatures exhibiting various levels of experience.)

If you suddenly and unexpectedly feel joy, don't hesitate. Give in to it . . . don't be afraid of its plenty. Joy is not made to be a crumb.

—MARY OLIVER[163]

Oliver ponders the questions: "Do stones feel?" Are trees delighted with themselves?[164] Her answer is an unequivocal "yes!" After all, as she witnesses the delight of a wren singing, what could such joy be if not prayer?[165]

Birds praise, roses sing, and all things have souls in this wondrous interdependent family of life. After catching and eating a fish, Oliver muses: "Now the sea is in me: I am the fish."[166] We are part of a lively, dynamic, constantly changing, perpetually perishing world, in which, despite our human uniqueness, we are connected with all that has gone before us, this present moment's unique blend of local and global, and future generations that will be shaped by our actions. Interdependence and experience are interconnected. An experiential universe is an enchanted, or re-enchanted, universe, in contrast to the disenchanted world of materialism, consumerism, and technological idolatry. We are part of Nature, continuous with the nonhuman world, and Nature is a part of us.

In this universe we are given two gifts: the ability to love and the ability to question. Which are, at the same time, the fires that warm us and the fires that scorch us.

—MARY OLIVER[168]

As she swims along the Cape Cod coast, Oliver remembers the "lost parts" of herself.[167] There is no "other"; our unique self is part of the ebb and flow of the ocean, the planet's seasons, and the galaxies beyond. Though each of us is unique in the universe, we are also permeable, part of a planetary and cosmic current that joins us with all things, reflecting and shaping all things, including God. This essential experiential empathy between the human and nonhuman worlds is evident in the experiences of mystics, poets, artists, and children.

The Body of God

Surprised by God's appearance in the Temple, Isaiah hears angelic voices chanting, "The whole earth is full of God's glory!" (Isaiah 6:3). On his way to work, Moses encounters God speaking from a burning bush. Confronted by otherworldly, body-scorning theologies that challenge Jesus' bodily existence, the author of John's Gospel asserts, "And the Word became flesh and lived among us, and we have seen his glory, the glory as of a father's only son, full of grace and truth" (John 1:14). God is as present in the world of the flesh, in the birds of the air, and lilies of the field, as in our "spiritual" lives. God is alive in the planetary rhythms and the human adventure. Each moment, even the most apparently ordinary one, is miraculous in its embodiment of Divine creativity and wisdom.

Oliver writes of the "god of dirt" that she finds in the voices of dogs, crows, frogs, and in the perpetually arising and perishing Holy Here-and-Now.[169] In the lively artistry of God, "Every morning the world is created."[170] God does something new each day, birthing the universe in every new millisecond—and every day, God is also something new.

Birth and death are both part of life in God's good world. Nothing lasts. Even death can praise God, as Saint Francis chants in his "Canticle of the Sun." This passing moment of beauty—this burst of life that defines our mortality—glorifies God and reveals the Heart of the Universe.[171]

As a process theologian, I affirm: "God in all things and all things in God." All things bear the imprint of Divine creativity and wisdom. "Cleave the wood and I am there,"

Jesus says in the Gospel of Thomas (77). "I am the vine and you are the branches," John's Gospel preaches (15:5). The sap of the vine flows through us, delighting in our fruitfulness and fecundity.

To those who locate God solely in scripture, institution, or steeple house, Oliver challenges: God is "the forest . . . the desert . . . the ice caps that are dying . . . the ghetto . . . the leaf of grass . . . [even] the politician . . . It could be that I am a tiny piece of God."[172] Inspired by Psalm 145—"On the glorious splendor of your majesty and on your wondrous works, I will meditate"—Oliver speculated that God's body is "everywhere and everything, shore and the vast fields of water."[173] When we discover a God-filled world, we are challenged to become artists of Divinity ourselves. Expressing our gratitude for God's abundant creativity, we plunge into a Divine world, using our gifts in partnership with the beauty of God in this holy yet passing moment of Divine fecundity.

> You too can be carved anew by the details of your devotion.
>
> —MARY OLIVER[174]

Prayerful Attentiveness

"Teach us to pray," asked the disciples of Jesus. Many of us ask that same question today. We grew up seeing prayers as one of three options: a matter of repetition, confession of sin, or petition for what we needed. By the time we reached adulthood, many of us concluded we had outgrown our childish understanding of prayer—and so we quit praying altogether. Others of us revert to old habits in times of crisis and uncertainty, pleading with a God whom we believe is in control of everything and can solve all our problems with the wave of the Divine hand.

Jesus did not intend for what later became known as the "Lord's Prayer" (or "Our Father" in Catholic circles) to be the only model for our prayer lives. Nevertheless, embedded in Jesus' prayer are elements of gratitude, forgiveness, awe and wonder, trust, petition, intercession, and ethical transformation, grounded in the affirmation that God's realm can be embodied "on earth as it is in heaven." The God Jesus described in his prayer is not a coercive all-determining Deity but a God who partners with humankind.

Author Anne Lamott described the elements of prayer as "wow, thanks, help,"[175] to which I would add "guide, inspire, and challenge." In whatever way we understand prayer, it is a form of what Jungian psychologists Ann and Barry Ulanov defined as "primary speech," expressing our relationship and dependence on powers greater than our own with whom we are intimately connected.

Mary Oliver does not give us a primer on prayer. In fact, she was careful not to define prayer but rather let prayer well up from experiences of amazement, wonder, tragedy, and concern. Spiritually, for Oliver, is an attitude toward life, an open receptivity to the holiness of the place and time. Her lines from "The Summer Day" reflect the experience of many seekers: "I don't know exactly what a prayer is," she wrote—and then affirmed her ability to pay attention.[176] After describing a scene of lilies, green moss, and rippling waters, Oliver noted that paying attention "is our endless and proper work."[177]

Confessing that she has not mastered the straight posture some identify with authentic meditative practices, Oliver described her own "meditative" technique, reminiscent of one of her poetic and spiritual guides Walt Whitman: "I prefer just to lounge under a tree." Yet, from the ambient openness of "lounging" comes the wonder of recognizing the world's mystery and beauty. What can we do but be amazed, and accept the miracle of the Holy Here-and-Now?

Attention without feeling is only a report.

—MARY OLIVER[178]

Still, our prayers are not entirely our own. In an interdependent universe whose holy energies of life and death and perpetual motion flow through us, we share in the prayers of the earth, sky, sea, and land. Our prayers participate, as Psalm 150 affirms, with snowstorms, breaching whales, roses bursting into blossom, and sharks on the prowl. Joined with all Creation, Oliver also felt power that lay outside herself and yet flowed through her.

Paying attention as a form of prayer affirms the wondrous, interconnected world that rises and dies with every moment's emergence. In paying attention, we discover eternity in our passing lifetimes, even in the short lifespan of the butterfly. We let go of permanence, trusting this moment in time as a revelation of Divine artistry. Even death, essential to the evolutionary process, becomes a blessing as we look beyond our limited ego and its needs to the wondrous interdependence of Life flowing through us.

Behold! There are burning bushes around every corner and thin places everywhere. God faithfully gives mercies anew every morning. Look! Listen! Taste! Touch! Smell! Imagine! Pay attention! You are on Holy Ground!

Attentive Prayer

Mary Oliver's poem "The Summer Day" has become a talisman for many of today's spiritual seekers. In my seminars, participants often close their eyes or nod their heads when I read Oliver's homage to the joys of spiritual meandering. The poem invites us to reflect upon the context and meaning of our lives, and to experience prayer in novel, inspirational, and provocative ways. In pondering the meaning of life, Oliver's gaze fixed on a humble grasshopper, whose process of chewing a blade of grass provoked her amazement and gratitude. Our human projects are not solitary, Oliver's poetry tells us, but part of a dynamic planetary journey, reflecting Divine creativity at the micro as well as macro levels.

Prayer, Oliver affirmed, is attentiveness to the rhythms of life flowing in and through us. Prayerfulness opens us to our unique experiences and the unique creatures with whom we interact. Prayer may not lift us to heaven, but instead, it brings Heaven to Earth in the ordinary affairs of life. Look! Behold! Open your senses! You are *always* on holy ground!

"The Summer Day" concludes with a question. It asks us to determine what we will each do with the precious life we've been given. This question always challenges me to look at my own life in a way that's similar to the traditional Ignatian Examen—the examination of conscience—as I consider where I stand in relationship to God and my personal and communal calling.

I invite you to reflect on "The Summer Day" in the spirit of *lectio divina*—holy reading. Read the poem twice, slowly and quietly. (You can find the poem online as well as in many of Oliver's collected writings.) Then, if weather permits, go on a prayer walk for at least ten to fifteen minutes, letting the poem's words shape your experience as you open yourself to the environment around you.

What do you notice?

Where do you experience beauty?

Are there any "grasshoppers" along your path? (If not a grasshopper, a firefly or butterfly, a rabbit, fox, robin, or any other living creature, no matter how seemingly humble?)

Where do you experience guidance? If something catches your eye, pause and notice, experiencing the uniqueness of your encounter with an insect, animal, plant, or tree.

Now, in the stillness, pose Oliver's question to yourself: "What do I plan to do with the amazing and wonderful life I've been given?" Without editing your response, let thoughts, dreams, or feelings emerge. Don't worry about concreteness or narrow realism. Let your imagination roam free. This form of self-searching is especially necessary in times of transition such as retirement, beginning college or a new job, becoming a parent, or facing a serious illness.

*Sometimes I need only
stand where I am
to be blessed.*

—MARY OLIVER[179]

Conclude this spiritual practice by journaling your insights. Make a commitment to explore what it might mean to embody some new possibility in your life.

Prayer of Our Spiritual Home

Creative Spirit, cleanse the doors of my perception
and open my senses that I might experience
the Infinity of everyday life.
Give me a sense of vision and purpose
that I might live my life with joy, courage, and compassion.

14

MAYA ANGELOU

Embodied Mysticism

We delight in the beauty of the butterfly,
but rarely admit the changes
it has gone through to achieve that beauty.

–MAYA ANGELOU[180]

We are all mystics. There is a mystic in everyone, and there is a mystic in you. We are all touched by God, whose amazing grace guides our steps even when we are unaware. Regardless of our personal history, God's loving providence brings us home even when we've lost our way.

Many people have stereotypes of saints and mystics. They perceive these folks as pure as the driven snow, immune to lust and anger, weak-kneed and meek, unconcerned with the scrum of political decision-making, their eyes always on heaven, even when they're making love. (Whoops! Mystics don't make love or have babies. Do they?) Or can we, in the spirit of the Song of Songs, experience God precisely in moments of physical pleasure and celebration?

Mysticism is multifaceted. It breaks down all our stereotypes. If God can be born in a manger, the child of working-class parents, living under the yoke of servitude, God can be born anywhere. God can be born in you!

The church father Irenaeus once asserted that the glory of God is a fully alive human! Along similar lines, a Jewish mystic said that when the Messiah comes, he won't ask if you were David—instead, he will ask, "Did you fulfill your personal destiny as God's image in human form?"

A mystic is someone who embodies the Spirit even in life's hubbub and furor. They are not perfect or immune to passion or sensuality, but instead, they bring everything they experience to God, seeking Divinity's healing touch and loving guidance. Mystics may be priests and pastors, but they are just as likely to be social workers or schoolteachers, bus drivers or bakers. Spiritual guidance may come from a monk; it may also come from a construction worker. Wisdom may come from a librarian or philosopher—and it may also come from an addict or a sex worker. God's vision

Try to be a rainbow in someone else's cloud.
Do not complain.
Make every effort to change things you do not like. If you cannot make a change, change the way you have been thinking. You might find a new solution.

—MAYA ANGLELOU[181]

embraces all of us, regardless of sexual expression, race, ethnicity, gender, or economics. God comes to us just as we are in all our wondrous imperfections.

Maya Angelou is truly a mystic for our time, a mystic of passion and embodiment. The morality police scorned her, and presidents praised her. She described herself—and other adventurous Black American women—as a "phenomenal woman."

Raised in the Episcopal Church, Maya Angelou was a wayward pilgrim. In her life's journey, Angelou found that God was always present, guiding her steps in all seasons and places. Indeed, her spiritual mantra in life's most difficult times was this: "There is no place where God is not." Not far off from human struggles or unconcerned with our personal stories, God is discovered in the very substance of becoming fully human—dancing, praying, and making love.

"A great soul serves everyone all the time," Angelou tweeted in 2016. "A great soul never dies. It brings us together again and again." Angelou herself was such a soul.

The Life of Maya Angelou

Maya Angelou (1928-2014) was a fully alive human who sought to experience wholeness and holiness embodied in the wondrous reality of life in all its tragic beauty and spiritual sensuality. Born Marguerite Johnson, her beginnings gave little indication that she would become a world-renowned writer, poet, speaker, and spiritual guide. After her parents' marriage collapsed when she was three years old, Maya and her five-year-old brother were shipped off by train with name tags affixed to their clothing, traveling alone from Los Angeles to their paternal grandmother in Stamps, Arkansas.

Growing up in the racially polarized South, young Marguerite had virtually no positive contacts with white people. Any interchange with white folks, even those less affluent or educated than themselves, could be perilous for Black Americans in the Jim Crow, Klan-ridden South. Looking back, Maya Angelou said, "If growing up is painful for the Southern Black Girl, being aware of her displacement is the rust on the razor that threatens the throat."[183] Like so many other young Black children at the time, Angelou recalled wanting "to look like one of the sweet little white girls who were everybody's dream of what was right in the world."[184]

> *You may not control all the events that happen to you, but you can decide not to be reduced by them.*
>
> —MAYA ANGLEOU[182]

When Maya was seven years old, her father took the children to live with their mother's family in St. Louis. There, young Marguerite received the name "Maya," from her brother's nickname for her: "Mya Sister."

In St. Louis, a boyfriend of her mother's sexually assaulted Maya; he threatened to kill her brother if she shared their secret. When she finally told her brother about the sexual abuse, the perpetrator was arrested, spent one night in jail, and then was mysteriously killed shortly after his release. With a child's sense of guilt, believing her words had killed the perpetrator, young Marguerite quit speaking and remained mute for years after. She feared her voice might harm other people if she felt negatively about them.

When she returned to her grandmother's home in Arkansas, her grandmother enveloped Maya in a circle of healing love. The old woman prophesied, much to the mute child's amazement, that Maya would have the opportunity to teach around the world. Such a prophesy seemed impossible to a frightened child—but to the Heart of the Universe, what we perceive as impossible is the womb of possibility. The Divine Life-Giver makes a way where there is no way.

At this time, she encountered teacher and family friend Mrs. Bertha Flowers, who in the context of her "lessons in living," mentored Maya in literature and poetry. Now, Maya woke up to her own giftedness as a writer and poet.

After the brutal murder of a Black man in their Arkansas community, Maya's grandmother took fourteen-year-old Maya and her brother to San Francisco to live with their mother. In her teens and twenties, Angelou became the first Black American to work as a streetcar conductor; she gave birth to a child, married and divorced a Greek man (Tosh Angelos from which the name Angelou emerged), danced in a strip club, was briefly a prostitute, ran a brothel, and took the first steps toward moving beyond a life of poverty and violence.

After relocating to New York, Angelou claimed her vocation as a dancer and singer, went on tour in Europe and Egypt as a member of the cast of *Porgy and Bess*, and participated in the Harlem Writers Guild. She married an African diplomat and freedom fighter, moved to Egypt and eventually to Ghana. When that marriage ended, she returned to New York, where she worked in Martin Luther King's Southern Leadership Conference and later became involved in the formation of the Organization of Afro-American Unity, under the direction of Malcolm X.

As a young mother, Angelou fell into a deep depression and could find no way out. Burdened by her struggles as a single parent, she reached out to her voice teacher, Frederick Wilkerson. He introduced her to the New Thought philosophy of Unity, and the power of affirmative faith transformed her anxiety into gratitude.

Wilkerson said to her: "See that yellow tablet? . . . See the pencil? . . . Now write down what you have to be thankful for." At first, she balked, but Wilkerson persisted, reminding her that she had something to live for and that despite her burdens, there was much for which to be thankful. Angelou wrote, "I picked up the pencil and began. 'I can hear. . . . I can write.' When I reached the end of the page, I began to feel silly. I was alive and healthy. What on earth did I have to complain about?"[186]

> *You may encounter many defeats, but you must not be defeated. In fact, it may be necessary to encounter the defeats, so you can know who you are, what you can rise from, how you can still come out of it.*
>
> —MAYA ANGELOU[185]

Throughout her life, Angelou continued to follow the practice she learned from Wilkerson. Always grateful for God's providential movements in her life, Angelou said, "The challenging days of my existence may or may not be bright and promising. I maintain an attitude of gratitude.

If I insist on being pessimistic, there is always tomorrow. Today, I am blessed."[187]

Malcolm X's assassination devastated Angelou, and for a short time, she returned to her singing career. A few years later, Martin Luther King recruited her to organize a march. This project was derailed when an assassin's bullet took King's life on Maya Angelou's fortieth birthday.

Despite her grief at King's death, Angelou's creative juices flowed as she wrote, produced, and narrated a PBS series on the connection between the blues and the African American experience. Shortly after that, she wrote her first autobiography, *I Know Why the Caged Bird Sings*, which brought her international acclaim.

In the years that followed, Angelou served as Lifetime Professor at Wake Forest University,; she directed films, acted in the television epic *Roots*, composed songs for Roberta Flack, and read her poem "On the Pulse of the Morning" at the inauguration of President William Jefferson Clinton. President Barack Obama honored her for her lifetime achievements as a poet and writer.

Maya Angelou had been nurtured in the church, where she witnessed the power of faith to provide courage and patience to face the daily indignities of racism. She experienced revival meetings in which farmworkers, housekeepers, and day laborers discovered their value as God's children. She found God's love in the arms of her grandmother, whose care and protection undergirded her future adventures.

Although Maya Angelou died in 2014, her life and her writing remain with us a witness to the power of faith. Despite racism, tragedy, and poverty, nothing could keep her from rising above the circumstances of life, guided by the vision that wherever she was, God was there. She went from humble beginnings to reading her poetry at a presidential inauguration and receiving the Presidential Medal of Freedom.

Rising Spirituality

Mystic Howard Thurman asked: How can a person develop healthy spirituality when their backs are against the walls and their spirits assaulted by racism, hatred, diminishment, and oppression? In his answer, Thurman noted that one of the greatest tragedies of poverty and oppression is the stifling of imagination among children.

How does the caged bird find freedom in the narrow confines of oppression? How do our spirits soar, discovering a way where there is no way, experiencing wholeness and holiness despite daily assaults on our dignity and selfhood from a violent and oppressive social order? For Thurman and Angelou, the sense of holiness—our own individual value—comes from within

This is a wonderful day. I've never seen it before.

—MAYA ANGELOU[188]

as well as beyond. Regardless of our social standing and the perceptions of others, we are God's beloved children of infinite worth. The voice of God, speaking from within our own hearts and minds and through our spiritual mentors, can drown out the voices of hate and fear.

In describing her spiritual undergirding, Angelou wrote:

We are all creative. We may have it beaten out of us, or kicked out of us, when we are children, or we may never have the chance to trust ourselves. But we all come from creator trailing clouds of glory. Imagine a slave sold to another person who has the right to say this person cannot move within one inch from where I can say he or she can move or can live or die if I say so. And this person says . . . , "I open my mouth to the Lord, and I won't turn back, no, I shall go, I will go, I'll see what the end is gonna be." Now that's a mystic. Daring! Imagine this, imagine. . . . "Go down Moses, way down in Egypt land. . . ." Imagine being sold by somebody and singing that. That's a mystic.[189]

Mystical experiences can occur during life's most dire situations. Prison walls could not stop the apostle Paul. Jail couldn't stifle the spirit of Martin Luther King Jr. Death threats didn't silence Malcolm X's message of dignity and pride. Rosa Parks wasn't scared of being arrested. Mystics discover they are part of a greater story, one the oppressor can't imagine.

You should be angry. You must not be bitter. Bitterness is like cancer. It eats upon the host. It doesn't do anything to the object of its displeasure. So use that anger. You write it. You paint it. You dance it. You march it. You vote it. You do everything about it. You talk it. Never stop talking it.

—MAYA ANGELOU[190]

"You may kill me," Angelou wrote, "but still, like air, I rise."[191] This "rising spirituality," enables us to embrace our pain and then transcend suffering through vision and affirmation.

Like people who rise above life's trials today, our ancient ancestors stepped out on God's word, trusting a higher power to empower them to do more than they could imagine. This rising is the movement of the Spirit, what Howard Thurman described as the "growing edge" that energizes and inspires us despite life's adversities and the limits we—and others—put on us, personally and socially.

> I thought if I wrote a book, I would have to examine the quality in the human spirit that continues to rise despite the slings and arrows of outrageous fortune. Rise out of physical pain and psychological cruelties. Rise from being victims of rape and abuse and abandonment to the determination to be no victim of any kind. Rise to be prepared to move on and ever on. I remembered a children's poem from my mute days that seemed to say however low you perceived me now, I am headed for higher ground.[192]

Maya Angelou's rising spirituality was grounded in her sense of God's providential all-sufficiency. The caged bird sings because no prison walls can truly bind her. Embodied and localized, fully in the moment, she is also eternal and infinite, marching forward from Egypt toward the promised land of Zion.

Angelou wrote that in even in the most difficult challenges, God's love "humbles me, melts my bones, closes my ears, and makes my teeth rock loosely in their gums. And it also liberates me," she went on to say. "I am a big bird winging over high mountains, down into serene valleys. I am ripples of waves on silver seas. I'm a spring leaf trembling in anticipation."[193]

Encompassing Spirituality

In many ways, Angelou's and my spirituality mirror one another, despite differences in the color of our skin. Both of us were raised in small-town, Bible-believing evangelical churches, where God was an abiding reality as near as your next breath. In those churches, we learned our well-being hinges on God's wise and miraculous care, which often makes a way where we perceive no way. Our wholeness is grounded in the "sweet hour of prayer" that enables us to live with adversity and begin again, despite the pain and mistakes of the past.

Love recognizes no barriers.
It jumps hurdles, leaps fences,
penetrates walls to arrive
at its destination full of hope.

—MAYA ANGELOU[194]

Neither Angelou nor I lost that gospel spirit as we matured, but both of us forged a lively sense of God's nearness through the creative synthesis of New Thought (later described as New Age spirituality), an affirmation of religious pluralism, and an ecumenical vision of global Christianity. We learned to live affirmatively, praising God all day long, knowing that God's eye is on the sparrow, God's grace is amazing, and we are always standing on God's promises.

In an interview with Oprah Winfrey, Angelou expressed the heart of her mystic vision. God is the All, she said. "There is no place that God is not, no place, in the prison, in the choir loft, on my knees, God is right there, God is All . . . all roads lead to God," who is the beginning and end of all things. "All roads"—eventually—"lead to God."

And, she said, the human soul is "the spirit that longs for All." This spirit brings forth from itself music, art, poetry. Her own poetry is grounded in the quest for truth that will lead us closer to All. In the spirit of a gospel hymn that she (like me) grew up with, she asserted: "Spirituality is surrender. I surrender all to All."[195]

This surrender to God's way involves saying, "Thy will be done," trusting that God's perspective and love are greater than our own. When we see dead ends, God sees vast horizons. Angelou's vision enabled her to glimpse God's providence in the challenges of racism, poverty, underworld violence, and drug use.

She admitted, though, that her faith was tested many times a day. When she felt hurt or betrayed or she experienced long-lasting pain, she said, she began "to doubt God and God's love." But—

Then the Spirit lifts me up again, and once more I am secured in faith. I don't know how it happens, save when I cry out earnestly I am answered immediately and am returned to faithfulness. I am once again filled with Spirit and firmly planted on solid ground.[196]

Once again, Angelou was heartened by an old, familiar gospel hymn:

> On Christ, the solid Rock, I stand;
> All other ground is sinking sand,
> All other ground is sinking sand.[197]

Wherever we are, Angelou asserted in the spirit of Psalm 139, God is with us; nothing in the whole universe nor any event in life can separate us from the love of God. If we ascend to the heights of ecstasy and amazement, God is there. If we descend to the depths of despair and are caught up in prostitution and unhealthy relationships, God is equally present. What we perceive as confusion and separation, is Light waiting to be seen.

God is not indifferent or impersonal; the Infinite cares for us the way a mother cares for her children. One of Angelou's most important moments occurred when a spiritual mentor, steeped in the Unity School of Christianity, challenged her to repeat "God loves me" throughout the day and whenever she felt her sense of personal value slip away. Angelou recalled:

I began to sense that there might be truth in that statement [God loves me], that there was a possibility that God really did love me. Me, Maya Angelou. I suddenly began to cry at the grandness of it all. I knew that if God loved me, then I could do wonderful things, I could try great things, learn anything, achieve anything. For what could stand against me with God, any person with God, constitutes a majority?[198]

Knowing God loves us enables us to rise above all the burdens that weigh us down. It liberates us from inner and outer oppression. It unites us with the beauty and energy of the vast God-filled universe. As Angelou proclaimed, "Stand up straight and realize who you are, that you tower over your circumstances. You are a child of God. Stand up straight."[199]

Sensuous Spirituality

When we realize a loving God guides, protects, and provides, we awaken to the glories of God in the world of the flesh. The heavens declare the glory of God—and so do our bodies, the texture and colors of our skin, the cells of our immune systems, our beating hearts, and the taste of good food. With the author of the Song of Songs, we can feel God's pleasure as we admire the beauty of our beloved, reveling in romantic love.

The horizon leans forward, offering you space to place new steps of change.

—MAYA ANGELOU[200]

God loves the world and that means our bodies, our sexuality, our parenting and grandparenting, our walking and running, eating and singing. Our body is the temple of the Spirit, and our senses are transparent windows into the

Divine. Mysticism awakens our physical senses to beauty and wonder. Incarnation blesses all the senses and every body.

As Angelou wrote:

> There are some that are so frightened by the idea of sensual entertainment that they make even their dwelling places bleak and joyless. And what is horrible is that they would have others share that lonely landscape. Personally, I'll have no part of it. I want all my senses engaged.[201]

While I know myself as a creation of God, I am also obligated to realize and remember that everyone else and everything else are also God's creation.

—MAYA ANGELOU[202]

God is the Great Entertainer, the Artist of Experience, whose beauty confronts us in every setting, whether we're walking down a city street, gazing at a sunset, admiring the beauty of our beloved, or transfixed by a jazz or symphony piece. We can experience God's creativity flowing through our own creativity, Divine poetry and artistry inspiring their own expressions. Amazement can be our response even on the most boring or challenging day, for God is in the world of flesh—in the color purple, a baby's soft skin, and the feel of our lover's skin. As author Bob Goff wrote, "The chemistry of God's love and our creativity work together when combined. No reservoir can hold it, no disappointment can stop it, and no impediment can contain it.

God has skin—and that skin is yours! No other spiritual path is as direct as the one that leads through your whole person, body, mind, and spirit. Spirit is sensuous and that enables you, regardless of your situation, to be a "phenomenal" human being.

Blessing and Being Blessed

Looking back at her life, Maya Angelou affirmed:

> Life is going to give you just what you put in it. Put your whole heart in everything you do, and pray, then you can wait.[203]

Sometimes, we may need medication to treat the physical causes of anxiety and depression; these psychiatric conditions can be very real physical illnesses. Even at such times, though, we can rise above our circumstances by remembering our blessings and choosing to bless others in return.

Many African American churches have a traditional prayer: "I thank you God for waking me up this morning. You didn't have to!" The gift of life one day at a time opens up an array of possibilities and adventures. As the author of Lamentations said:

> *The steadfast love of [Yahweh] never ceases,*
> *. . . mercies never come to an end; they are new every*
> *morning; great is your faithfulness.* (3:22–23)

God is faithful and provides a way where there is no way. Gratitude opens our spirits to providence, as well as our own abilities to change our life circumstances. We may have suffered abuse as a child; we may experience discrimination and hatred in our lives; but still, with Maya Angelou, we can *rise*. Even on the darkest day of our lives, we, like Martin Luther King in Birmingham's jail, might even write something that helps to change our world.

When we "count our blessings," naming them "one by one" (as the old hymn goes), we may be surprised to discover not only what "God has done," but what *we* could do to heal the world and bless others.

In this exercise, begin with a time of quiet prayer, calming your spirit and centering your mind on God's providential care. After a few minutes, ask God to reveal to you the many blessings you are already receiving.

Then, take out a pad of paper or your computer, and list your blessings. Pause and give thanks for all you have received personally, relationally, and because of the circumstances of your birth (to your particular family, with your particular skin color, in your particular community).

> *Stormy or sunny days, glorious or lonely nights I maintain an attitude of gratitude.*
>
> —MAYA ANGLEOU[204]

Next, ask God to reveal ways you can bless others, both today and over the long haul. List possibilities for blessing. This morning, for example, I noted simple ways I can bless others:

- Be more attentive to my wife's needs. Listen better to her.

- Give full attention to my grandchildren and listen for the emotions beneath their words and actions.

- Smile and give a good word to people I randomly meet on my walks and as I travel around town.

- Write a check to an organization that supports human rights.

- Be attentive to injustices I observe and respond to them with creative love.

- Share my time and wisdom with my grandchildren.

- Be a mentor to young people, ministerial students, and aspiring writers.

- Phone my political representatives regarding environmental and justice issues.

When we count our blessings, living by what Maya Angelou described as an attitude of gratitude, we discover we are truly blessed—and out of our blessings, we can bless others.

Prayers of Our Spiritual Home

Holy One, give me a heart of gratitude.
Let me count my blessings, constantly giving thanks
to you and those around me.
Let my heart swell with joy at your care and abundance.
Out of my blessings, let me bless others.
Guide me to people and situations
where I can share your love and healing presence.

15

MYSTICISM AND THE HEALING OF THE NATION'S SPIRIT

Awakening to Our Better Angels

Sacred Activism is the fusion of the mystic's passion
for God with the activist's passion for justice,
creating a third fire, which is the burning sacred heart
that longs to help, preserve, and nurture
every living thing.

—ANDREW HARVEY[205]

Mystics give us a vision of what human life can be. They go from self-interest to world loyalty, affirming our connections with one another and the human and nonhuman cosmos. Their vocation is to become co-workers—albeit humble and fallible co-workers—in God's quest to heal the spirit of our nation and the planet. They demonstrate that the heights of mystic experience give new perspectives on life, revealing that our spiritual GPS orients us toward justice.

The thirteen mystics described in this text would have recognized the wisdom of Unitarian Universalist pastor and abolitionist Theodore Parker's vision of the universe and, by implication, America:

> I do not pretend to understand the moral universe, the arc is a long one, my eye reaches but little ways. I cannot calculate the curve and complete the figure by the experience of sight; I can divine it by conscience. But from what I see I am sure it bends towards justice.[206]

Each mystic in this text intuited a deeper reality than meets the eye, a deeper naturalism and morality that outlasts injustice and violence and calls each of us to seek that "more perfect union," both in our nation and our spiritual lives.

Certain individuals, including the thirteen American mystics celebrated in this text, are unique in gifts, graces, and commitment. This allows them to plumb the heights and depths of experience, and glimpse the far horizons of Divine and human possibility. These mystics show us what it is like to be alive and lively, experiencing the glory of God.

Mystics' experiences have transformed them—and then they go out and tell others about those experiences! These visionary women and men reveal to us our deepest destiny, what we can become through the grace of life and human responsiveness. They tell us we can experience the same vision that inspired their spiritual adventures, and they provide us with open-spirited pathways and possibilities to become their companions on the spiritual quest.

All the great religions of the world have their origins in individuals' extraordinary encounters with the Holy. At their best, the great religions promote a democracy of revelation and human fulfillment. While the history of religions is ambiguous, given as much to pettiness as grandeur, persecution and violence as compassion and healing, the religious adventure, lured forward by mystics in every era, helps guide the spiritual and moral arcs that call individuals and communities to live in alignment with all that is good and healthy.

Like great religions, a great nation begins with a great vision. This vision often emerges from insights greater than those who initiated the vision, mere mortals who are torn by the ambiguities of life and their own self-interest. Though often short-sighted and selfish, the spirits of all nations are energized by the possibilities of what humankind can become in community.

The United States is no exception. The nation's founding documents aspire to a new humanity, embodying novel possibilities for the human adventure. These affirmations continue to call our nation to greatness:

> We hold these truths to be self-evident, that all men are created equal, that they are endowed by their Creator with certain unalienable Rights, that among these are Life, Liberty and the pursuit of Happiness.

These foundational words chart the outlines of a political democracy that's undergirded by belief in a democracy of revelation and the affirmation of humanity in all its diversity. Although enslaved and Indigenous people and their descendants can rightly say, with Langston Hughes, "America was never America to me," we can also hope, often against hope, for America to be, as Hughes also wrote, "the dream that dreamers dreamed," where all breathe the air of freedom, equality, and access to abundant life.

The thirteen mystics in this text reveal both a universal and uniquely American mysticism. They revel in what humankind can become, freed from the chains and limitations of falsehood, inequality, and self-forgetfulness. They see the human spirit as unbounded, revelation as universal, and value as ubiquitous.

Freedom and human rights emerge from our affirmation of revelation as universal. Enlightenment and creativity, self-sacrifice and ecstasy, belong equally to the children of people who were enslaved and the children of slaveholders. The vision may be aspirational rather than concrete at any unique moment in U.S. history, but the democracy of Divine revelation connects us—even when we are unaware of it—in the quest to build the Realm of Heaven on Earth.

These thirteen mystics—and authentic mystics everywhere—were not content with the status quo, nor did they accept the current state of our nation as final. Their mysticism was restless and passionate, sometimes given to prophetic challenge of structures of injustice and violence. They wanted everyone to share in life's fullness in body, mind, spirit, and political and personal agency. Their patriotism was cosmopolitan, joining love of nation with love of the whole Earth in its diverse cultures, nations, and creatures.

The mystics in this text were grounded in their faith traditions, whether Indigenous, Jewish, or Christian. Their commitments to their home religions, however, were often held critically and with a dose of skepticism, taking them beyond stale and narrow creeds, life-denying orthodoxies, and anemic visions of salvation. They saw the Divine everywhere and in all people, and they explored ways the nation itself could become a laboratory for the human adventure.

The mystic, as Howard Thurman counseled, must become a social critic, recognizing and then challenging everything that blocks the way

The fact that modern physics . . . is now making contact with mysticism, the essence of religion . . . shows very beautifully the unity and complementary nature of the rational and intuitive modes of consciousness; of the yang and the yin.

—FRITJOF CAPRA[207]

to human wholeness. Though mystics seldom set out to be prophets, each of our thirteen individuals sought a "more perfect union," decried inequality and injustice, and sought freedom for all God's children. Many were harshest in their condemnation of their fellow worshippers, recognizing that religion is often employed to bolster injustice, dishonesty, and demagoguery (in both the nineteenth and twenty-first centuries).

Mysticism, in the American spirit, leads to personal and political transformation. Mystical experiences do not devalue history but plunge us into the clamor of historical conflicts and the policies that promote hate, incivility, and injustice. Even the most introverted of mystics, Emily Dickinson, saw well beyond her Amherst village to embrace the horizons of wholeness to which all humans are entitled. These mystics had faith in the future, although their eschatology was gentle and evolutionary rather than violent and abrupt.

Our dreams of a new world order will not come to pass unless we become God's partners in healing the world. Nor can our visions be fully realized unless all of us are included. The hoped-for embodiment of God's realm "on earth as it is in heaven" must have room for General Custer as well as Sitting Bull, Bull Conner as well as Martin Luther King Jr., white supremacists as well as Black Lives Matter supporters, Donald Trump as well as John Lewis. Even Judas will be welcomed back to Jesus' agape feast.

> *Mysticism joins and unites; reason divides and separates.*
>
> —THOMAS STEPHEN SZASZ[210]

Each of these mystics affirmed that all life is miracle. Each day was a revelation to them of the Divine Spirit in human flesh, the wondrous diversity of humankind, and the beauty of the ambient nonhuman world. Mystic experiences broadened their horizons and invited them to experience the Holy everywhere and in everyone—and then act in the light of that vision in personal relations and political advocacy.

These mystics were called to *see* the light of the world and then *be* the light of the world. They continue to remind the United States that its spiritual destiny is to be a light on a hilltop, illuminating not only the privileged but also the humble, forgotten, and broken, the people who are the victims of our nation's false and self-interested priorities.

The reality that God's love equally embraces all nations does not excuse America from being exceptional in the sense of being exemplary in its quest for justice and the willingness to sacrifice national interests for global well-being. As President Joe Biden said, "We lead not by the example of our power, but by the power of our example."[209]

Agony and ecstasy come together in the radical empathy of these Earth-affirming mystics. Mysticism leads to celebration, as it also awakens us to others' suffering. Alfred North Whitehead's description of God as "the fellow sufferer who understands" also applies to the people Divinity has touched.

Our thirteen American mystics celebrated the wonder of life, even as they also felt the despair of poverty, the hopelessness of injustice, the anger of marginalization, and the demonic spirit of racism and political demagoguery that stifle the human spirit and undermine the nation's destiny as a place of liberty and justice. These individuals aspired toward a time when God will "crown our good with [deep kinship] from sea to shining sea."

In this third decade of the twenty-first century, amid the changing position of the United States in an intricately interconnected world, as our nation is fraught with internal danger as well as external threat, we must accept the reality that we are all—or we must become—mystics of the American spirit. Rooted in the knowledge that we are no better than the mystics of other lands, we must nevertheless fulfill our unique spiritual vocation in this challenging time. Loving our land while honoring others' love for their own countries, we affirm the democracy of revelation that inspired our national parents, despite the ambiguity of their actions and failures to embody all the truths they proclaimed.

Today's mystics, like the good ancestors who encountered the Holy throughout the American experience, know Divinity energizes us all. Despite the fraying of our common bonds as Americans, we must listen for the mystic chords of kinship that transcend race, class, party, gender, sexual expression, age, and nation of origin. We can be transformed and united—and then shout it to the mountain tops. We are bound together in an intricate tapestry of interconnection in which one and many are joined in constant transformation.

Now more than ever, we need to claim the transcendent vision of these thirteen (and many other less well-known) American mystics. These American visionaries show us the contours of the vision of

We have been the recipients of the choicest bounties of Heaven; we have been preserved these many year in peace and prosperity; we have grown in numbers, wealth, and power as no other nation has ever grown. But we have forgotten . . . the gracious hand which preserved us in peace and multiplied and enriched and strengthened us, and we have vainly imagined, in the deceitfulness of our hearts, that all these blessings were produced by some superior wisdom and virtue of our own.

—ABRAHAM LINCOLN[211]

what we may be, if we choose, as individuals and as a nation. They point us toward the far horizons of Earth-care and liberty and justice for all. They remind us to see the holiness of one another and affirm the interdependence that makes our nation great. They challenge us to incarnate the democracy of revelation in the realization of democratic principles in the voting booth and courthouse. They inspire us to value otherness and expand the circles of justice to embrace everyone. They take the law seriously, while reminding us that beyond inflexible adherence to law is a Higher Law that's energized by love.

Only a politics of love can save us. This love must be embodied in respect, commitment to the common good, and the willingness to sacrifice for causes greater than ourselves. There is hope for America if we attend to these mystic chords.

Healing the spirit of the nation is still possible, despite the stresses that purveyors of prevarication and destroyers of democracy have placed on it. The voices of our inner angels call us to higher ground, where we can be shining lights of justice and freedom, beacons of hope for the planet. Uplifted by our contact with the spiritual realm, we will be empowered to walk in step with the mystics I've described in this book.

Together, we will discover we each have our own mystic melodies to sing. Arm and arm with these thirteen mystics, whether marching in protest or on our knees in prayer, we will climb the path to higher ground.

May God make it so.

Prayer for Our Nation

Let us then rest humbly in the hope
authorized by the Divine teachings,
that the united cry of the Nation
will be heard on high, and answered with blessings,
no less than the pardon of our national sins,
and the restoration of our now divided
and suffering Country.
(Abraham Lincoln[212])

NOTES

1. Vernon Howard, *Mystic Path to Cosmic Power* (West Nyack, NY: Parker Publishing, 1967), 11.

2. Howard Thurman, Mysticism and Social Action: Lawrence Lectures and Discussions with Dr. Howard Thurman (London: International Association for Religious Freedom, 2014), Kindle location 235–236.

3. The Anthropic Principle is the hypothesis, first proposed in 1957 by Robert Dicke, that the range of possible observations that could be made about the universe is limited by the fact that observations could happen only in a universe capable of developing intelligent life.

4. Richard D. Robinson, *Emerson: The Mind on Fire* (Berkeley: University of California Press, 1995), 126.

5. "Concord's Irreparable Loss," Concord Library, https://concordlibrary.org/special-collections/emerson-celebration/Em_Con_78.

6. Throughout this book's scripture quotations, the publisher has chosen to replace "the Lord" with the more accurate (and less patriarchal) "Yahweh," the name Divinity claimed in conversation with Moses in the Book of Exodus. Bible scholars indicate that this mysterious name has several possible meanings, including: Life-Giver, Self-Existent One, the One who brings into existence everything that exists, and the One who creates the order of universe.

7. Robinson, 69.

8. Ibid., 179.

9. Laura Dassow Walls, *Henry David Thoreau: A Life* (Chicago, IL: University of Chicago Press, 2017), xv.

10. Robert D. Richardson, Jr., *Henry Thoreau: A Life of the Mind* (Berkeley: University of California Press, 1997), 285.

11. Walls, 81.

12. Richardson, 389.

13. Walls, 228.

14. Ibid., 304.

15. Ibid., 89.

16. Robinson, 76.

17. Ibid., 119.

18. Walls, 131.

19. Ibid., 347.

20. Ibid., 347.

21. Henry David Thoreau, *Walking* (San Bernardino, CA: Cricket House, 2018), 1.

22. Ibid., 1.

23. Ibid., 3.

24. Ibid., 20.

25. Ibid., 34.

26. Ibid., 36.

27. Justin Martin, *Rebel Souls: Walt Whitman and America's First Bohemians* (Philadelphia, PA: Da Capo Press, 2014), 189.

28. Ibid., 194-195.

29. Thich Nhat Hanh, *Peace Is Every Step* (New York: Bantam Books, 1991), 123-124.

30. W. H. Auden, *For the Time Being: A Christmas Oratorio* (Princeton, NJ: Princeton University Press, 2013), 65.

31. The sixteenth-century mystic Ignatius of Loyola created the "Examen" as a tool for regularly assessing our spiritual well-being.

32. Cynthia Griffin Wolff, *Emily Dickinson* (Cambridge, MA: Perseus Publishing, 1988), 4.

33. James McIntosh, *Nimble Believing: Dickinson and the Unknown* (Ann Arbor: University of Michigan Press, 2004), 64.

34. Ibid., 1.

35. Roger Lundin, *Emily Dickinson and the Life of Belief* (Grand Rapids, MI: Eerdmans, 2004), 91.

36. Early Christian mystics defined kataphatic spirituality (the way of affirmation), which emphasizes beauty that is revealed and apparent, and apophatic spirituality (the way of negation), which dwells on the Divine glory that remains concealed, hidden from view. The poet Henry Vaughn, who wrote from both perspectives, used the phrase "a deep and dazzling darkness" in his poem "The Night."

37. McIntosh, 54.

38. Lundin, xiv.

39. McIntosh, 104.

40. Kirstin Lemay, *I Told My Soul to Sing: Finding God with Emily Dickinson* (Brewster, MA: Paraclete Press, 2013), 87.

41. Thurman, 235–236.

42. David Sox, *John Woolman: Quintessential Quaker* (Richmond, IN: Friends United Press, 1999), 1–2.

43. Janet Whitney, *John Woolman: American Quaker* (Boston: Little, Brown and Company, 1942), 29.

44. Richard Frances, *Mother Ann: The Story of Ann Lee, Female Messiah, Mother of the Shakers, the Woman Clothed with Sun* (New York: Arcade Publishing, 2000), 48.

45. Ibid., 48.

46. Nardi Reeder Campion, *Mother Ann Lee: Morning Star of the Shakers* (Hanover, NH: University Press of New England, 1990), 76.

47. Ibid., 82.

48. Ibid., 66.

49. Ibid., 85.

50. Campion, 37.

51. Robley Edward Whitson, *The Shakers: Two Centuries of Spiritual Reflection* (New York: Paulist Press, 1983), 226.

52. Frances, 124.

53. Campion, 43.

54. Whitson, 268.

55. Suzanne Skees, *God Among the Shakers: Search for Stillness &
    Faith at Sabbathday Lake* (New York: Hyperion, 1999), 172.

56. Campion, 141.

57. Shaker Museum, https://www.shakermuseum.us/collection/
    break-every-yoke-shakers-gender-equality-womens-suffrage/
    spirit-and-body/mother-ann-lee.

58. Skees, 183.

59. Shaker Museum

60. Ibid.

61. Campion, 122.

62. Boris Boyko, "Ann Lee, a Woman of Great Faith," *Liberty*
    (January/February 2014), https://www.libertymagazine.org/
    article/ann-lee-a-woman-of-great-faith.

63. The Oglala are one of the seven tribes of the Lakota people.
    Many Oglala reject the name "Sioux," given to them by white
    men, because it may have come from a derogatory word that
    meant "snake."

64. For a survey of the "historical" Black Elk, see Jon Sweeney,
    Nicholas Black Elk: Medicine, Catechist, Saint (Collegeville,
    MN: Liturgical Press, 2020).

65. Harry Oldmeader, *Black Elk: Lakota Visionary* (Bloomington,
    IN: World Wisdom, 2018), 104.

66. Joe Jackson, *Black Elk: The Life of an American Visionary* (New
    York: Picador, 2016), 15.

67. Joseph Epes Brown, *The Sacred Pipe: Black Elk's Account of
    the Seven Rites of the Oglala Sioux* (Norman: University of
    Oklahoma Press, 1989).

68. Brown, xx.

69. Oldmeadow, 11.

70. Brown, 53.

71. Donald Worster, *A Passion for Nature: The Life of John Muir*
    (New York: Oxford University Press, 2008), 319.

72. Ibid., 424.

73. John Muir, *Atlantic Monthly* (April 1898).

74. Worster, 55.

75. Right whales are currently the most endangered whale on Earth. This is mostly due to human-caused deaths, which exceed the birth rate of new calves. The two biggest threats to right whales' survival are being struck by boats and getting tangled in commercial fishing gear. And with climate change altering ocean ecosystems, these whales have turned up in new places at unexpected times, making it more difficult for them to feed and more difficult for existing measures to protect them.

76. John Muir, *John of the Mountains: The Unpublished Journals of John Muir*, Linnie Marsh Wolfe, ed. (Madison: University of Wisconsin Press, 1979), 299.

77. Gil Bailie quoting a personal communication with Thurman in *Violence Unveiled: Humanity at the Crossroads* (Chestnut Ridge, PA: Herder & Herder, 1996), 276.

78. For more on contemplative activism, see Bruce Epperly, *Prophetic Healing: Howard Thurman's Vision of Contemplative Activism* (Richmond, IN: Friends United Press, 2020) and *The Work of Christmas: The Twelve Days of Christmas with Howard Thurman* (Vestal, NY: Anamchara Books, 2017).

79. Thurman, *With Head and Heart* (New York: Harcourt and Brace, 1979), 9.

80. Ibid., 7.

81. Ibid., 226.

82. Ibid., 15–16.

83. Quoted in Luther Smith, *Howard Thurman: The Mystic as Prophet* (Richmond, IN: Friends United Press, 2007), 35.

84. Howard Thurman, *Mysticism and Social Action: Lawrence Lectures and Discussions with Dr. Howard Thurman* (London: International Association for Religious Freedom, 2014), Kindle location, 109.

85. Ibid., Kindle location, 113–114.

86. Ibid., Kindle location, 116–117.

87. Ibid., Kindle location, 177–179.

88. Ibid., Kindle location, 235–236.

89. Ibid., Kindle location, 249–251.

90. Ibid., Kindle location, 270–274.

91. Howard Thurman, *Deep Is the Hunger: Meditations for Apostles of Sensitiveness* (Oakland, CA: Eucalyptus Press, 2007), 24.

92. Howard Thurman, *A Strange Freedom: The Best of Howard Thurman on Religious Experience and Public Life* (Boston: Beacon Press, 1999), 248.

93. Ibid., 104.

94. Howard Thurman, *Meditations of the Heart* (Boston: Beacon Press, 2014), 211.

95. Luther Smith, *Howard Thurman: The Mystic as Prophet*, 127.

96. Howard Thurman, *A Strange Freedom*, 300.

97. Howard Thurman, address given at Spelman College (Atlanta, SC: May 1980).

98. Abraham Joshua Heschel, *Man Is Not Alone: A Philosophy of Religion* (New York: Macmillan, 1976), 270.

99. Although we often think of prophets as people who can foretell the future, the biblical meaning of a prophet is one who speaks the truth (even when it is uncomfortable or painful) to their community.

100. Abraham Joshua Heschel, *Moral Grandeur and Spiritual Audacity* (New York: Farrar, Straus and Giroux, 1997), 296.

101. The Baal Shem Tov—which means "Master of the Good Name"—is a name used for Israel ben Eliezer, an eighteenth-century Jewish mystic and healer who is regarded as the founder of Hasidic Judaism.

102. Moses Mendelssohn was a German-Jewish philosopher and theologian whose writings and ideas were a central element in the development of the Haskalah—the "Jewish Enlightenment"—of the eighteenth and nineteenth centuries.

103. Edward K. Kaplan, *Abraham Joshua Heschel: Mind, Heart, Soul* (Philadelphia, PA: Jewish Publication Society, 2019), 101–102.

104. Susannah Heschel, in *Abraham Joshua Heschel: Essential Writings* (Maryknoll, NY: Orbis, 2011), introduction.

105. Heschel, *Abraham Joshua Heschel: Essential Writings* (Maryknoll, NY: Orbis Books, 2011), 17.

106. Edward K. Kaplan, *Spiritual Radical: Abraham Joshua Heschel in America* (New Haven, CT: Yale University Press, 2007), 132.

107. Heschel, *Moral Grandeur and Spiritual Audacity*, 276, 296.

108. Heschel, *I Asked for Wonder* (New York: Crossroads, 1983), vii.

109. Ibid., 3.

110. The Hebrew words here are usually translated as "Lord of Hosts," with the "hosts" often assumed to be a group of warriors. Abarim Publications' Biblical Dictionary, however, says this traditional translation would indicate that God is the God of warfare, but a more accurate translation, based on how the same word is used elsewhere in the Hebrew scripture, would be that God is the God of organization and cooperation.

111. Kaplan, *Spiritual Radical*, 203.

112. Ibid., 60.

113. Heschel, *I Asked for Wonder*, xii.

114. Ibid., 153.

115. Heschel, *No Religion Is an Island: Abraham Joshua Heschel and Interreligious Dialogue*, Harold Kasimow, ed. (Maryknoll, NY: Orbis Books, 1991), 27.

116. Heschel, *Moral Grandeur and Spiritual Audacity*, 262.

117. Heschel, *The Prophets*, Volume 2 (Peabody, MA: Hendrickson Publishers, 2014), 3-4.

118. Heschel, *Moral Grandeur and Spiritual Audacity*, 296.

119. Ibid.

120. Heschel, *Man Is Not Alone: A Philosophy of Religion* (New York: Macmillan), 174.

121. Heschel, *Essential Writings*.

122. Heschel, *The Prophets*, 19.

123. Heschel, "Religion and Race," speech given on January 14, 1963.

124. Heschel, *Essential Writings*.

125. Heschel, *Moral Grandeur and Spiritual Audacity*, 76.

126. Heschel, *The Sabbath*, 8.

127. Ibid., 3

128. Ibid., 22.

129. Heschel, *Moral Grandeur and Spiritual Audacity*, 258.

130. Madeleine L'Engle, *Walking on Water: Reflections on Faith and Art* (New York: Convergent, 2016), 172.

131. L'Engle, *Genesis Trilogy* (New York: Shaw Books, 2001), 48.

132. Bruce Epperly, *I Wonder as I Wander: The Twelve Days of Christmas with Madeleine L'Engle* (Vestal, NY: Anamchara Books, 2018).

133. L'Engle, *Walking on Water*, 359.

134. L'Engle, *A Stone for a Pillow* (New York: Convergent, 1986), 198.

135. L'Engle, *Walking on Water*.

136. L'Engle, *Two Part Invention: The Story of a Marriage* (New York: Open Road Media, 2016), 79.

137. Quoted in Sarah Arthur, *A Light So Lovely: The Spiritual Legacy of Madeleine L'Engle* (Grand Rapids, MI: Zondervan, 2018), 169–170.

138. Ibid., 186.

139. L'Engle, *Walking on Water*, 78.

140. Arthur, 101.

141. L'Engle, *Bright Evening Star: The Mystery of the Incarnation* (Wheaton, IL: Shaw, 2001), 30.

142. Ibid., 21.

143. Ibid., 32.

144. Ibid., 167.

145. L'Engle, *Walking on Water*, 109.

146. L'Engle, *The Wrinkle in Time Quintet* (New York: Macmillan, 2013), 400.

147. L'Engle, *Genesis Trilogy*, 52–53.

148. L'Engle, *A Ring of Endless Light* (New York: Macmillan, 2008), 172.

149. L'Engle, *Genesis Trilogy*, 11.

150. L'Engle, *Walking on Water*, 75.

151. L'Engle, *Genesis Trilogy*, 10.

152. L'Engle, *Walking on Water*, 45.

153. L'Engle, *A Wind in the Door* (New York: Squarefish, 2007), 99, 109

154. L'Engle, *Walking on Water*, 41.

155. Mary Oliver, *Red Bird Poems* (Boston: Beacon, 2008), 28.

156. Oliver, *The Leaf and the Cloud* (New York: DeCapo Press, 2000), 10.

157. Oliver, *Devotions: The Selected Poems of Mary Oliver* (New York: Penguin, 2017), 105.

158. Oliver, posted on her Facebook page on September 17, 2016.

159. Oliver, *Upstream: Selected Essays* (New York: Penguin Books, 2016), 10.

160. Ibid.

161. Mary Duenwald, "The Land and Words of Mary Oliver, the Bard of Provincetown," *New York Times* (July 1, 2009), https://www.nytimes.com/2009/07/05/travel/05oliver.html

162. Ibid.

163. Oliver, *Devotions*, 68.

164. Ibid., 24.

165. Ibid., 47.

166. Oliver, *New and Selected Poems, Volume One* (Boston: Beacon Press, 1992), 165.

167. Ibid., 172.

168. Oliver, *Winter Hours* (New York: Houghton, Mifflin, Harcourt, 2000), 45.

169. Oliver, *Devotions*, 343.

170. Ibid., 345.

171. For more on Saint Francis, see Bruce Epperly, *Walking with Francis of Assisi: From Privilege to Activism* (Cincinnati, OH: Francis of Assisi, 2021).

172. Oliver, *Devotions*, 87.

173. Ibid., 136.

174. Oliver, *Long Life: Essays and Other Writings* (Boston: De Capo, 2005), 98.

175. Anne Lamott, *Help, Thanks, Wow: The Three Essential Prayers* (New York: Penguin, 2012).

176. Oliver, *Devotions*, 316.

177. Ibid., 264.

178. Oliver, interview with Krista Tippett, *OnBeing*, October 15, 2015.

179. Oliver, *Owls and Other Fantasies: Poems and Essays* (Boston: Beacon, 2006), 35.

180. Maya Angelou's Facebook page, post from May 15, 2013.

181. Angelou, *Letter to My Daughter* (New York: Hachette, 2010), 7.

182. Ibid., 5.

183. Angelou, *The Collected Autobiographies of Maya Angelou* (New York: Random House, 2004), 9.

184. Ibid., 7–8.

185. Angelou's Facebook post on May 1, 2009.

186. Angelou, *The Collected Autobiographies*, 610–611,

187. Claudia Abbott, "Maya Angelou Sings Songs of Love," *Science of Mind* (www.scienceofmind.com/e-mail/2014/pdf/MayaAngelou_January_2014.pdf), 10.

188. Angelou's Facebook post from December 16, 2010.

189. Angelou, The Collected Autobiographies, 8.

190. Interview with Melissa Harris-Perry, Elle Magazine (March 9, 2018)

191. Angelou, *Maya Angelou: The Complete Poetry* (New York: Random House, 2015), 159.

192. Angelou, *The Collected Autobiographies*, 1067.

193. Angelou, *Wouldn't Take Nothing for My Journey Now* (New York: Random House, 1993), 73.

194. Angelou's Facebook post on December 17, 2013.

195. Interview with Oprah Winfrey on *Supersoul Sunday*, Episode 416, May 19, 2013, http://www.oprah.com/own-super-soul-sunday/soul-to-soul-with-dr-maya-angelou-part-1-video.

196. Angelou, *Wouldn't Take Nothing for My Journey Now*, 33–34.

197. Edward Mote, 1834.

198. Angelou, *Wouldn't Take Nothing for My Journey Now*, 75.

199. Angelou's Facebook post on January 30, 2013.

200. Angelou, Presidential Inaugural Ceremony (Washington, DC: January 21, 1993).

201. Angelou, *Even the Stars Look Lonesome* (New York: Random House, 1997), 36.

202. Angelou, *Wouldn't Take Nothing for My Journey Now* (New York: Bantam, 2011), 18.

203. Angelou, *I Know Why the Caged Bird Sings*, 264.

204. Angelou, *Letter to My Daughter*, 32.

205. Andrew Harvey, *Radical Passion: Sacred Love and Wisdom in Action* (Berkeley, CA: North Atlantic Books, 2012), 490.

206. Theodore Parker, *The Collected Works of Theodore Parker* (London: Trübner, 1863), 48.

207. Fritjof Capra, *The Turning Point: Science, Society, and the Rising Culture* (New York: Bantam, 1983), 47.

208. Howard, 17.

209. Joe Biden, speech given on November 7, 2020, in Wilmington, DE.

210. Thomas Stephen Szasz, *The Untamed Tongue: A Dissenting Dictionary* (Chicago: Open Court, 1993), 233.

211. Abraham Lincoln, Proclamation Appointing a National Fast Day (March 30, 1983).

212. Ibid.

MORE BOOKS BY BRUCE EPPERLY:

God Online

A Mystic's Guide to the Internet

Perhaps the world is saved one act, one click, or one post at a time.

When we do ordinary things with great love, as Therese of Lisieux counseled, we bring beauty and healing to our companions on the Internet and to the planetary mind. The omnipresent God is as near as the next key stroke, the next post or response to another's online comment. We need a whole-person spirituality grounded in a sense of the holiness of all creation and reverence for life, despite the conflicts that characterize our world—and given the amount of time most of us spend online, we need to include these activities in our spiritual lives.

Bruce Epperly guides his spiritual Internet manual with the wisdom of

the Christian mystical tradition. These insights, both ancient and modern, help us to claim our vocation as God's companions in healing the world—through the vehicle of social media and other online interactions. Each chapter's dialogue with a mystic concludes with a spiritual practice that enables us to discover, in the spirit of the patriarch Jacob's exclamation, that "God is online, and we did not know it."

Become Fire!
Guideposts for Interspiritual Pilgrims

In the spirit of God's call to creative transformation, Bruce Epperly invites you to join him on a holy adventure in spiritual growth, inspired by the evolving wisdom of Christianity and the world's great spiritual traditions, innovative global spiritual practices, and emerging visions of reality. Epperly explores the many resources of Christian spirituality in dialogue with the spiritual practices of the world's great wisdom traditions, describing the gifts other spiritual paths contribute to the pathway of Jesus; at the same time, he uses the lens of the spiritual practices Jesus has inspired throughout Christian history to examine these spiritual paths.

Epperly write as a Christian committed to Jesus, whose teachings and way of life he believes lead to pathways of healing and creative personal and planetary transformation. By embracing the diverse insights of spiritual wisdom givers, physicists, cosmologists, healing practitioners, and Earth keepers, we can meet the Earth's current challenges with love, joy, and a united strength.

Jesus

Mystic, Healer, and Prophet

Who do you say Jesus is?

In his answer to this age-old question, Bruce Epperly brings us a new vision of Jesus of Nazareth, the healer, mystic, and prophet who is always more than we can imagine. This Jesus embraces all times and places with his mystical union with God, his healing presence, and his transforming prophetic challenge.

Rather than requiring supernatural intervention from outside our reality, the Jesus of the Gospels is present in the natural, ordinary-yet-amazing world we too inhabit. The energy of his love opens up new realms of unexpected possibilities within our daily lives. At the same time, he

points the way to meeting the challenges of our broken world. He calls us to venture out beyond the safe boundaries of doctrines and institutions, into new adventures of spiritual growth and inclusive ethical imagination. The quest to know Jesus never ends—and yet at the same time, he lives in us, inspiring us to embrace the ever-present God and transform the world.

From Cosmos to Cradle

Meditations on the Incarnation

This book takes its inspiration from the familiar Gospel Nativity stories—but it is far more than a Christmas book. As we revisit the characters of the familiar Christmas stories, we are invited to a new understanding of the Incarnation. We realize that, like Mary, we too are called to be the wombs and midwives of Divine revelation. We may receive Divine guidance and inspiration in dreams, just as Joseph did, and like him, find the courage to go against our society's expectations. Like the shepherds, we are welcomed to see the ongoing glorious pageant of God-made-flesh. And finally, we learn from the magis' example to widen our spiritual horizons and explore new paths.

In Jesus, the Word is made flesh; God has skin, cells, a reproductive system, and circulatory system. Our own souls and cells also reveal God's artistry, for they too embody the Source of all life. In fact, incarnation is everywhere we turn, revealing the marriage of Creator and creature in all its messiness.

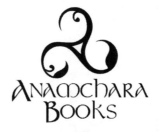

Anamchara
Books

AnamcharaBooks.com